words on target

words on target

For Better Christian Communication

Sue Nichols

Art by Doyle Robinson

JOHN KNOX PRESS • Richmond, Virginia

Second printing 1964

Library of Congress Catalog Number: 63-16410

© M. E. Bratcher 1963

Printed in the United States of America

2186 (20) 7014

Do You Agree?

"The greatest sin is to be dull."

Jack Paar, TV personality

"If only the preacher would remember that dullness is fail-ure . . ." George A. Buttrick, minister and author

"I have a vast and terrible desire never to bore an audience."

Billy Wilder, movie producer

"Some of us are altogether too much inclined to claim for this truth which is God's the hearing it deserves; and always it gets only the hearing *we can win for it*."

Paul Scherer, minister and author

". . . if . . . words are to enter men's hearts and bear fruit, they must be the right words shaped cunningly to pass men's defences and explode silently and effectually within their minds."

J. B. Phillips, minister and author

. . . if so, read on

This book is designed for

       ministers

       directors of Christian education

       church school teachers

       missionaries

       youth advisors

       women's leaders

       men's leaders

       lecturers

       writers

       and *all* who wish to communicate more effectively with twentieth-century Americans.

Contents

19TH Versus 20th

Paul wrote the Colossians, Season your speech "with salt" [1]; had he been writing today, he might well have advised "with Tabasco sauce!"

For the old Greeks had only theatres, occasional orators, and hard-to-come-by scrolls with which to compete. But today's would-be communicator contends with NBC, CBS, ABC, billboards, magazines, paperbacks, marquees, records of all sorts, and a zillion other distractions. Dead lies the Sunday evening church service, mortally wounded by radio and given the *coup de grâce* by Ed Sullivan. And pity the missionary whose mimeographed letter arrives in the same mail with the *Ladies Home Journal* or the *Saturday Evening Post*.

Not only does today's preacher, speaker, writer, or teacher face more competition, but he also faces twentieth-century competition. That is, he either says his "it" in an up-to-date fashion or he doesn't say it at all as far as his audiences (or readers) are concerned.

For communication underwent a distinct change at the turn

of the century. The audience reaction to the Hiram College Showboat demonstrates it. During the summer months, the drama students of the college sail the old "Majestic" down the Ohio River re-enacting once-new melodramas. Titles like *Murder in the Red Barn, Ten Nights on the Barroom Floor,* and *Lust, Lucre, and Liquor.*

The students present the plays faithfully. The lines are unaltered. The director and the stagehands duplicate the staging and costuming of the old-timey productions; the actors imitate the mannerisms and gestures of the bygone performers to the best of their ability.

When the curtain goes up, the audience beholds a series of utter tragedies. Drunken fathers squander their families' meager paychecks; virtuous daughters fend off the bold advances of brutish villains; untried youths spill their blood to preserve their family's honor. Almost every conceivable misfortune finds enactment on the showboat's stage.

And yet every performance is a romp for the actors and a sidesplitting experience for the audience. Everyone disembarks the boat at the end of the evening feeling he has witnessed a hilarious comedy.

In direct contrast, Joyce Cary tells us how similar plays were received in the 1800's. His hero, Chester Nimmo, says:

> I was trembling all over. My face was wet with tears and sweat. I heard myself utter groans and smothered cries. It was all I could do not to shout out my sympathy and my rage. In fact cries of anger and exclamations of horror did continually break out from the audience throughout the whole performance. The women, especially, gave vent to their feelings. The old wife who had admitted me to the ropes never stopped muttering to herself, "Ah, poor thing—poor old man—listen to the brute, and he a gentleman born." One girl, also near the ropes, broke into loud hysterical sobs.[2]

One audience doubles up with laughter; the other spends itself in weeping. One audience labels what it saw "humorous"; the other labels it "heartbreaking." Yet the plays are the same; only the times have changed. The times, and how we impart serious words to one another.

Amusement is a typical reaction to what is old-fashioned. We laugh at a bustle; we laugh at the "flickers"; we laugh at a Model T. We do the same thing with old books, documents, letters, and speeches. When the wife of the vicar of Wakefield cries out: "The vile strumpet has basely deserted her parents without any provocation; thus to bring your grey hairs to the grave, and I must shortly follow" [3]—we can't help it, we grin! Such formal oratory streaming from a supposedly heartbroken woman strikes us as ludicrous.

But we are not always amused. The genius of the Hiram Players lies in their ability to make dreadful, essentially non-communicating drama pay off. They are uniquely lucky. Most efforts to foist dull, out-of-date material on Mr. and Mrs. Jones run headlong into modern irritation or, worse, chilly disdain.

The story is told of a practical joker seeking retribution on his enemy. In a quaint bookstore he found a huge, musty old volume with a vague title. Quickly he bought it, wrapped it, and sent it to the man he disliked. Along with it he dispatched a message: "I disagree with this author's criticism of you," he wrote and signed the name of one of his enemy's colleagues. Pride drove the recipient to labor through the whole tome—in vain.

Now, in this account the typical American sees the ultimate in revenge. No other act—be it poisoning, dueling, stealing the man's wife—could afford us the chortles this one does, so thoroughly annoying looms the thought of reading anything dry and passé.

A literary critic, looking back over the prose of Theodore Dreiser, writes: "Unfortunately, he had no more selectivity than a glacier, and pebbles and boulders alike were carried forward in that unrelenting march." [4] The sentence bristles with modern irritation. The critic begrudges the hours he gave Dreiser and wishes he'd read Hemingway instead.

Yes, laughter and vexation—and now we come close to the third reaction to non-modern communication: the cold shoulder, the turned back.

Americans have their own built-in winnowing systems. They have to have: They are bombarded from all sides with slogans, catchwords, and singing commercials from morn to night. Like Eliza Doolittle in *My Fair Lady* they sometimes feel like crying out, "Words, words, words; I'm so sick of words." Even free toothpicks in restaurants come wrapped in sealed, sanitary sales' spiels these days.

In such an environment men have had to learn to distinguish the interesting from the tedious quickly or drown in the deluge. And distinguish they do. Rumors say that during certain peak television viewing hours, city reservoirs drop while the commercials are on. This rings true whether it is fact or not. For commercials, repeated *ad nauseam,* bore people, and they escape to their kitchens for glasses of water. Their community imbibition registers at the local utility station, even if not on Madison Avenue!

Most attempts, then, to communicate with Americans in a non-modern fashion encounter laughter, resentment, or indifference.

NIMMO IS DEAD

Yes, Chester Nimmo who sweated out *Murder in the Red Barn* is dead. His descendant sits in the pew and the rush-hour bus. And the sooner Christian communicators begin shaping their messages for him, the better.

For we want to be *heard,* not ignored. We want full churches and crowded classrooms. We want our magazines read, our lessons absorbed, our sermons acted on, our books studied, our appeals fulfilled. What good is wallflower Christianity?

Furthermore, we do not want to offend by our style. We must offend often enough by our content; why compound the problem? We must speak to men of sin, suffering, and death. We must ask them to relinquish their sovereign hold on their lives. We must tell them that God requires their time, their energies, and their money. These truths will never win any popularity contest. Yet they are imperative. Surely we will never encourage men to receive them by long, vague, trite harangues. By presentations that grate on their nerves or give them the fidgets.

George Buttrick denounces dullness as "a breach of love"[5]; and his description fits. For when we refuse to imbue our communication with freshness and zest, we say to others, in effect, "I don't care a fig about you." When we ask men to wade through thoughts carelessly assembled or page after page of bland platitudes, we disclose our essential indifference to them.

Finally, we want our content taken *seriously*. Sunday school lessons that provoke giggles, whether audible or repressed, degrade the faith. And sermons so pompous they generate snickers bring disgrace to the gospel. Our communication ought to build up the church, not bring down the house!

Humor has its place; Jesus used it often. We don't laugh out loud at some of the things he said (as his immediate audience undoubtedly did) only because we can't translate his phrases into vernacular American-English quickly enough; humor depends on timing for much of its effect. We read "whited sepulchres"[6] as if Jesus were pronouncing some sort of benediction upon the Pharisees instead of calling them a "bunch of spruced-up tombstones."

Humor has its place: We use it to slice open hypocrisy, to keep our audience awake, to disarm our critics. But its place is always subordinate. We are funny to accomplish some end other than being funny. We are missionaries, not comedians.

All of which leads us to the question: Who is our audience? Who are our readers? What is Nimmo's descendant like? If we are to shape our communication for him, we had better understand his characteristics. He has several attributes, but three particularly concern the Christian communicator.

SOPHISTICATED, FREE, DISTRACTED

Our man is sophisticated, free, and distracted.

He is sophisticated. If he is not city- or suburban-bred, he is on his way to being so. Statistics indicate a depopulation of our farmlands. The country yokel is joining the smart set. He is the fruit of a several-generation-public-school-system, and his comprehension and tastes manifest it.

American sophistication frequently shows up clearly in certain facets of the Cold War. *Holiday* magazine carried an article recently by a Chinese journalist, who obviously knew Western readers very well. She recounts her visit to Shanghai, saying: "I tell him [Comrade Liu] that Shanghai is like a woman whose first marriage was a mistake, and who has decided to remarry, this time with the right person.

"But this figure of speech doesn't please Comrade Liu. He is angry at my frivolity. He wants me to see Shanghai as the Chinese I meet speak of it: as the old capitalist, imperialist city, now regenerated, purified, cleansed of its sins and its old vicious ways, the past buried forever; facing the future with a Boy Scout resolution, with new factories and steel plants and textile mills, and a wide green belt of parks around its ten new satellite cities. And sexually pure. He says that there has been a three-in-one revolution in Shanghai: the physical revolution, a great cleanup; the political revolution, mass re-education, new industries and the Great Leap Forward; and the moral revolution, a liquidation of corruption and vice. The people of Shanghai, once corrupted by the West, are now joyously entering the new life.

"I tell Comrade Liu that I cannot write of Shanghai that way, that no one would read such a revivalist tract.

"'Why can't you write it that way?' says Comrade Liu, for the fifth time. 'It is only the truth.'

"I try to explain that in a capitalist society the nervous, defensive style, the declamatory justification, do not sound as convincing as facts put in a deprecatory manner. 'People want to laugh at the same time as they weep,' I say . . ." [7]

Facts put in a deprecatory manner, understated or expressed with subtlety, convince Western readers because they are sophisticated. The peasant, like the country boy, may believe in facing the future "with Boy Scout resolution"; the citified American is highly skeptical.

He is also free. Free to tune the communicator in or out at will. Free to pour over or to wastebasket our leaflets and tracts.

Free to drive to the country or take to the golf links on Sunday morning.

And even when he shows up at church he is still free. He has not necessarily come to worship or be instructed. Some are there to impress the boss, some to pursue a romance, some to show off a new fur coat. A quiet congregation is not per se a listening congregation; everybody may simply be off gathering his own wool.

For Americans are a busy, distracted lot. A myriad activities and worries vie for their attention. Which has made them a nation of master dippers. They seldom pick up a book with the thought "I will now concentrate on this." Instead they dip. They read the first sentence or the first paragraph (in extreme cases, as when waiting for a train, the first page) to see if it "sounds interesting."

They dip with even greater delight into magazines, for periodicals are usually illustrated so that little or no reading is required. If the pictures "look interesting," they buy one.

Newspapers are expressly tailored for dipping. Journalists cram all the important facts into the first sentence of their stories so that you need not read further (unless, of course, you *saw* the accident or your child was *in* the pageant).

But even as they dip, the readers are apt to be thinking of something else: not "I will read this article," but "The baby-sitter is late again" or "As soon as I get home I'm going to get out of these shoes."

How many women listen to sermons, minds half on the words and half on the roast at home; their name is Legion. And how many people sit through Sunday school classes still trying to put together last night's mystery story or juggling the prospects of what to do in the long afternoon ahead?

Americans are sophisticated, free, and pressured. If we hope to reach them with the good news of Christ, we must communicate in a strictly twentieth-century manner.

The Big Three

What is a strictly twentieth-century manner of communicating? With what qualities must we endow our works if they are to attract and hold our audiences?

Time and again—in investigations of popular books, shows, movies, and magazines—three qualities emerge. Aside from the content itself, they make the material or presentations appealing. They are economy, energy, and subtlety.

ECONOMY

Economy means communicating without any unnecessary words. It means saying things quickly, using short words in short paragraphs. It means quitting on time even if we must sacrifice the third point.

Before 1900, communication trudged from author to receiver on a great mass of words. In Thomas Godfrey's play *The Prince of Parthia*, one of the characters cried out, "Hence from my sight —nor let me, thus pollute mine eyes, with looking on a wretch like thee, thou cause of all my ills; I sicken at thy loathsome presence." [1] Today he would shout, "Scram!" and let it go at that.

No literary embroidery for modern Americans. They want to catch the message or at least the beginning of the message on the fly. They appreciate the communicator's economy of their time through the economy of his writing.

Not only are the passages short in modern works, so are the words. "Pretentious words bring a certain self-consciousness, which makes for a cold reception," says Norman Shidle in *Clear Writing for Easy Reading*.[2] Thomas Hardy described an oat-harvest taking place under a "monochromatic Lammas sky," [3] in *Far From the Madding Crowd*. A twentieth-century Hardy would call it (simply) "blue."

Just as the mind shys at long words, so it balks at drawn-out works in general. Ministers are often praised for their sermons on the sole basis that they were short. A few of our denominations recognize this thirst for brevity. Abingdon Press recently issued a Know Your Faith series for laymen. Although the books are hardbacks, these are typical lengths: *I Believe in the Holy Spirit*, 89 pages; *I Believe in the Bible*, 77 pages; *I Believe in God*, 62 pages. Hardbacks in The Layman's Theological Library (The Westminster Press) run like this: *Believing in God*, 94 pages; *The Significance of the Church*, 96 pages; *Understanding the Bible*, 94 pages.

Indeed, language, to some extent, is going out of style. Consider how much is conveyed by the so-called method actors, like Marlon Brando, through sounds and gestures rather than words. In the film *Beloved Infidel*, Deborah Kerr and Gregory Peck went from sitting at a table trying to ignore one another to dancing in each others' arms, without a single word of dialogue passing between them. Many lines in modern plays are not sentences at all, only fragments. One drama critic, reviewing *Come Back Little Sheba*, commented on how much Shirley Booth conveyed by the way she *stirred her coffee* in one scene.

Audiences and readers, alert and receptive to today's economical communication, can comprehend a great deal without seeing it or hearing it in words.

Energy means communicating with force. It means propelling our thoughts into the minds of others. It means girding our message in strong, vivid language so that what we say "registers."

Baxter Hathaway cautions that ". . . communication often fails simply because the reader does not feel the impact of the writer's mental energy. Energy of writing supplies the momentum for the transmission of many difficult ideas across the barrier of a reader's inattention." [4]

An author of the past wrote for ready readers: men and women who had uncluttered minds and schedules to give him. Therefore, he made little or no effort to generate his thoughts beyond the printed page. Vague phrasing, limp verbs, trite sentiments bothered him not at all. Indeed, they were in good taste. For the communicator's job was to keep the reader's mind on the right track, not to rip open his own. So writers kept a polite distance from their works. And today's reader catches no sense of mental ferment, author-involvement, "brain-strain" back of their words.

But today's communicator must ensnare dippers: He must arrest the attention of men and women on the go. He cannot remain detached and aloof. "A man may write on Love and Art and Peace and what not," says Charles Horton Cooley, "but he will write to little purpose unless he has, back of it all, a *natural ferocity*." [5]

Two paragraphs may help us see this quality of energy. Both deal with the subject "humility." The first one appeared in a recent issue of the *Reader's Digest;* the second is from an early work in the 1900's called *Christian Ethics for Daily Life:*

Humility

It does not saturate a personality, but flavors it. Theodore Roosevelt was a man of immense tempo, something of a bull in a china shop at times, barging exuberantly into almost every avenue of life. Yet he could say cheerfully, "Nobody can accuse me of having a charming personality"—a remark much closer to true humility than a long face and a pious bringing together of the finger tips. The late Fiorello La Guardia, New York's colorful mayor, was famous for his candid acknowledgment of a blunder: "When I make a mistake, it's a beaut." Neither of these men confused humility with dimming his own light; rather, admitting the voltage, they could also admit that it was sometimes ungovernable.[6]

   . . . humility and kindred virtues are the starting point—the basis of Christian character. Only the docile, listening, eager spirit of a child is ready for the truth and for growth and entrance into the Kingdom. He that would be greatest shall be servant of all. Except ye become as little children ye cannot enter the kingdom of heaven. The son of man came to minister. "To be without self-importance, to be humble, simple minded, trustful, receptive, to be content with lowliness and let all else be great" is the spirit of the kingdom. To develop such a moral character is to realize one's highest self.[7]

The first paragraph exudes energy. The writer contends that humility flavors personality. He then summons up two specific examples to prove his point. Americans know that neither Theodore Roosevelt nor Fiorella La Guardia were dolts. By selecting a quotation from each of them that expresses humility, the writer makes his point effectively. Note that he gives the sources of his quotes and states what the men said exactly. He doesn't leave the matter vague: "Some of our national leaders were men of humility and made humble statements." The modern reader would throw up his hands with the cry, "Good grief! Who were they and what did they say?"

Furthermore, the writer uses strong writing techniques. His verbs have substance: "saturate," "flavor," "confuse," and "admit." His phrasing is apt and colorful: "immense tempo," "barging exuberantly," "pious bringing together of the finger tips," "dimming his own light," "admitting the voltage." The words quickly conjure up meaning for modern readers, enticing them to go on with the article.

In dreary contrast, the second paragraph lacks energy. The writer's contention seems to be that humility is the basis of Christian doctrine. But his proof is vague; for the modern reader, almost nonexistent. The second sentence is but a longer restatement of the first. The next three sentences come from the Bible and do, to be sure, enjoin us to be humble. But the writer doesn't enclose them in quotation marks or tell us their biblical origin. He thereby robs them of an authority they might otherwise enjoy. (He probably assumed his readers would recognize them as Bible verses, but such an assumption, even in his day, was risky.) The sixth sentence contains quotation marks, but no source is given. The reader doesn't know whether St. Augustine, the kaiser, John Doe, or the author himself said it. Since it reads like a longer version of the second sentence which is simply a longer version of the first sentence—the original contention—it does nothing (without a spelled-out source) to convince the reader. The last sentence is utterly trite.

The verbs throughout the whole paragraph pall. Other than the borrowed biblical verbs "came" and "enter," the writer uses only "to be," the weakest verb in the language. The virtues "are," the spirit "is," he "shall be," to be without "is," and to develop "is." The modern reader soon tires of this blandness and returns *Christian Ethics for Daily Living* to its dusty shelf. He must have more zest!

Subtlety means communicating without overdrawing conclusions for the receiver. It means putting facts together with such artistry and restraint that listeners grasp our point without our coming right out and telling them. It means giving our surface material a subsurface power, understood but not articulated.

Mark Hellinger, in his commandments for writing, put it: "A writer is the eyes, ears and nose of the reader—the reader is his own brain."[8]

Comments on modern productions by critics and others reveal the attraction of what is subtle. "She draws the fine line between sentiment and sentimentality,"[9] wrote Brooks Atkinson, drama critic of the *New York Times,* in praise of actress Margaret Sullavan.

Louise Townsend Nicholl lauded a volume of poetry by Sara Henderson Hay: "This is a lovely work—but lovely has too light a sound! Only a strong undertow puts such a spume upon the beach."[10]

Again, on the dust jacket of Anne Morrow Lindbergh's *Gift from the Sea* we read: "She does this without the overtones of preaching, but herself as a seeker, echoing—only clearer and stronger—our own small still voice."[11]

The most obvious difference between the communication of yesteryear and today lies in this area of subtlety. Most old works of literature strike us as artificial and overdone.

Consider, for example, two poems. The first one is an anonymous selection from *Poems with Power to Strengthen the Soul* (1907) compiled by James Mudge. The second is from E. B. White's *The Second Tree from the Corner*, 1954 edition:

Summer and Winter

If no kindly thought or word
    We can give, some soul to bless,
If our hands, from hour to hour,
    Do no deeds of gentleness;
If to lone and weary ones
    We no comfort will impart—
Tho' 'tis summer in the sky,
    Yet 'tis winter in the heart!

If we strive to lift the gloom
    From a dark and burdened life;
If we seek to lull the storm
    Of our fallen brother's strife;
If we bid all hate and scorn
    From the spirit to depart—
Tho' 'tis winter in the sky,
    Yet 'tis summer in the heart![12]

Disturbers of the Peace*

The cows lie sweetly by the pond,
    At ease, at peace (except for flies);

---

* "Disturbers of the Peace" from *The Second Tree from the Corner* by E. B. White. Copyright 1939 by E. B. White. Originally appeared in *The*

The glassy morning waves its wand
And bids the summer day arise.

Arise, O pesky day, arise!
The peaceful cow, with flies
to bother,
The dog his worms, the hen her
lice,
And Man—Man his eternal
brother.

Both poets aim to lay bare and rebuke man's deep-seated selfishness. But how differently they go about it!

The first writer tells all. He plunks black and white down in front of us in no uncertain terms. Black in eight lines; white in eight lines. As soon as the mind grasps the meaning of the words, it can retire. For the poet has done all our thinking for us; we need only listen. Listen and reform. And in reforming we know exactly what to do: say kind words, do deeds of gentleness, lift burdens, etc., etc. It's all set down for us.

Not so with the second work. No advice, no maxims, no formulas-for-living sprawl before the reader. The poet goes about his work like a saboteur. On the surface he presents a scene of innocent calm and naturalness. But all the while he is unloading dynamite.

To keep us reading he drops hints along the way that more than "daybreak on the farm" is at stake, but they are only hints. At the outset of the second stanza he begins to plant the charge. His tight, short phrases build suspense. Soon he lights the fuse. And then, with the quick thrust of the last line, he tears a great hole in our unsuspecting complacency.

When the dust settles, the reader still has work to do. He stands exposed. His egotism swirls before him as a far uglier proposition than making "winter" in "summer." He must do something. Many people read the poem again to see if they can't get it to say something else. But whatever they do, they are on their own. Mr. White has hit and run. He has acted as

---

New Yorker, and reprinted with the permission of Harper & Row, Publishers, Incorporated.

ears for us to hear our own mean salute to the day, but he well knows "the reader is his own brain."

CONCLUSION

Economy, energy, and subtlety, then, pry open twentieth-century American minds. They convert dippers into readers. They are the "open sesame" to the deeper and often troubled recesses of modern beings.

The rest of this book deals with what communicators can and should do to give their efforts these imperative qualities. Almost all untrained writers and speakers make the same basic mistakes. To avoid them requires two things: (1) a recognition that they are indeed mistakes and (2) initial disciplined effort to steer away from them. In other words, the rules for better communication are simple, but they cannot be taken lightly. However, anyone who follows them will automatically improve what he has to say!

Not Yet

Good communication begins in the mind. Not on paper, not in the typewriter, and *not* before an audience. It begins in the mind of the communicator: in certain attitudes and thought processes that precede the issuance of words. Three such processes are particularly important. (1) Bottle up your message long enough to give it power. (2) Approach your assignment as a human being. (3) Assume no ready-made audience.

1. A DAMMING-UP PROCESS

Water carries a built-in drive to reach the sea. Given half a chance it trickles out of its mountain haunts and begins tumbling down the hillsides.

A drive also animates ideas and emotions: a drive to escape the human body and gain expression in the air or print. This similarity gives us a valuable clue concerning power.

Left to itself, water bobbles along over sticks and stones, dissipating its potential, piecemeal. But when men fling a dam across its course, the chaotic flow is checked. Energy blends with energy as the water from many rains backs up behind the spillways. At the right moment, a gate opens at one side and a turbulent wave plunges down the flume. It socks the waiting turbines with terrific force. Power breaks forth, not as raw water but as electricity—performing on behalf of man.

When amateur communicators say the first thing that comes to mind, their material pours out in long, wordy sentences with featherweight verbs and trite, obvious sentiments.

As the babble continues, it gets more and more confusing. Second-rate ideas consume more time (or space) than the first-rate. Participles dangle. Pronouns lack antecedents. Main thoughts end up in subordinate clauses. Past, present, and future tenses chase each other. Subjects do not agree with their predicates. Whatever zest the original message had, it soon dwindles away.

A skilled communicator dams up the initial flow. He curtails it until he can sort out his precise message. Until he can phrase it with strength and release it in an altered but more powerful form. You can see it in the expressions that follow: the sense of an "original" that is held back until it can be carefully refined.

Catherine Marshall (commenting on writing of her husband's death):

> Not only did I have to re-experience every vivid detail in order to transfer it to paper, but there was the necessity of holding that emotion in check. I am convinced that real communication in writing always has to be disciplined. It is never achieved either by stickly sentimentality or by careless diffusiveness. Trying to attain anything approaching this ideal was like attempting to rein in a pair of runaway horses—exhausting at best.[1]

Mark Hellinger: "The way to write a sob story is to be callous."[2]

Paul Scherer: "Speak with moderation, but think with great fierceness."[3]

The grief that came with a death, the blatant sob story, the fierce thought—all are held in check. For good communication begins where will power thwarts the exit of premature ideas and cheap words. Where open emotion is given time to veil itself. Where stray thoughts are given time to circle the reservoir of general knowledge. There energy blends with energy. There powerful communication breaks forth—performing on behalf of God and man.

You may have to hold back your message for years, especially if it is complex or foreign to your experience. On the other hand, you may need to dam it up only briefly. Only long enough to unskein the sinews of thought and sheath them in hearty nouns and verbs.

Just don't hurry into composition.

2. IMPART, DON'T IMPUGN

Attitude two: Approach your assignment as a human being. Don't write or speak down to your receivers as if you were Stylites up on a pedestal, nearer heaven. James Sellers, in speaking of the attempt to write and speak in the language of the man of the street, says: "It is not a matter of popularizing, or of watering down the gospel, or of speaking or writing in a condescending way to the laity; it is a job which demands the best minds in the church but which has all too often been mismanaged by the poorest." [4]

Use technical terms and in-group jargon sparingly, so that you need not define constantly. Watch out for over-use of such phrases as: you ought to, this means that, let me remind you, you must, you need to be aware of, and everyone knows that . . .

Vary your sentence structure. An unending stream of simple, declaratory sentences belongs in a reading book for the first grade; in adult communication it is insulting. Put two clauses together and give your reader a compound sentence. Subordinate less important matters for an occasional complex sentence. Dust off a question or two. Toss in some dialogue, imaginary if necessary.

An outline can insult, too. Especially since the eye usually traces it through first. Consider this fairly typical example of work. The outline, all on the first page, reads:

Resource Guide for a Unit of Material

I. Significance and Scope of the Unit
   (one typing space follows)
   A. Significance of This Unit
      (an indented paragraph follows)
   B. Scope of This Unit
      (an indented paragraph follows)
II. How to Use This Guide

It should read:

Resource Guide for a Unit of Material

I. Significance and Scope of the Unit
   A. Significance
   B. Scope
II. How to Use Guide

Since no other unit or guide is mentioned or hinted at, the repetition of "This Unit" and "This Guide" only demeans the reader's intelligence. Be generous; assume that your readers can follow an orderly, simple discussion.

From time to time use household, nonreligious words. Dr. Buttrick begins one of his sermons: "The Bible offers its truth not in cellophane, but in flashes of drama."[5] How marvelous! Here is a theologian who knows about cellophane.

Inserting "secular" words in *printed* material is particularly crucial. Modern readers often scan the page before they settle down to the first sentence. If they see nothing but "grace," "creed," "doctrine," and "sin," held together by "is's" and "was's" they will set your message aside.

What's wrong with letting people know you look at TV, read *Time* magazine, "Pogo," or Nero Wolfe? Drop a few names not associated with the church. So-called outsiders often say surprisingly pertinent things. Lucille Ball said: "There seems to be something lacking in our education in this country. We don't put enough emphasis on genuine happiness. We train our children how to do complex jobs, how to get ahead, and how to accomplish all manner of clever things, except maturity. Maybe instruction in how to grow up gracefully should start in our teens. Youngsters should be made aware of what satisfactions they want in life and how to go about getting them. Not just material success, but maturity, self-esteem, the love you give to and get from children—the attributes of real happiness."[6]

That's not quite Horace Bushnell, but it's not bad.

3. WIN INTEREST

Attitude number three: Assume no ready-made audience. Nothing so beguiles us into insipid expression as the casual confidence that men want to hear what we have to say. Don't believe it. *No*body is automatically interested in our message. We cannot even assume that our audience or readers are automatically interested in God's message. Regardless of how important, sacred, or controversial our content, we must begin beckoningly. Paul Scherer says God's truth "gets only the hearing we can win for it."

Too many preachers and teachers behave like female anglers. You know how it is with the average woman. The thought of picking up a live, wiggly worm and jabbing a hook through it sends shivers down her spine. And the thought of sticking lively, red-blooded words into their sentences chills many Christian communicators.

Indeed, the whole business of providing a lure for their would-be public repels them. To be assertive, imaginative, different, or humorous in order to attract listeners or readers seems unnecessary. "The fish are there and waiting," they maintain. "Just let down the line, wait a bit, and then reel away."

Ah, the fish may be there, but they are not myopic; they know a naked hook when they see it. And they aren't going to impale their interest on our drabness while hundreds of fancier prospects swim by.

Or, "The fish are weary of frills," the non-communicator declares. "Give them a simple message from the heart and they will respond." (Which sounds admirable.) But usually such messages, when they come out, sound more like they originated instead in the area of the soft palate. Or at least from somewhere *between* the mind and the heart. For they lack sufficient grist to set us thinking or sufficient drama to trigger our emotions.

If by a message from the heart we mean something like Psalm 130—fine! ("Out of the depths I cry to thee, O Lord! Lord, hear my voice!") But if we mean a tepid concoction of generalities, a string of sentences that look like they came from a drowsing committee—then fie!

Begin, then, interestingly and tellingly; as if you had to create concern for your theme out of a vacuum. Begin:

- with something pithy (Gigantic, citified aggregations will dominate tomorrow's world.)
- with a quotation ("I lost God in a Sunday school class,"[7] Mildred Whitcomb tells us.)
- with a little-known fact (Pretzels are supposed to remind us of Christ's passion.)
- with an intriguing lead-in (Five great lies plague modern man.)
- with a word origin ("Heathen" derives from the people "who lived on the heath."[8])
- with a nagging question (Can a working mother maintain a Christian home?)
- with a play on words ("Conscience: Something that no's what's wrong."[9])
- with a startling statistic (The average American is now confronted by over *one thousand five hundred* ad impressions daily![10])

Do not begin:

- with elaborate acknowledgments or thank-yous (Get on with what you have to say.)
- with a series of irrelevant jokes (Unless you are speaking to juniors or at a church picnic.)
- with a lament over the brief time given you to deal with the subject at hand (You simply make the time *more* brief!)
- with an apology of any sort for the poor presentation you are about to make (The audience will not forgive you anyhow.)
- with "it is" or "there are" (They tell us nothing.)

A speech may commence at a slightly slower pace than something printed. People need time to look you over and adjust to your voice. For example, in print, I just said, " 'Heathen' derives from the people 'who lived on the heath.' " However, had I been speaking, I would have inserted "The word" in front of "Heathen," so that the sentence would come out "The word 'heathen' derives from the people 'who lived on the heath.' "

If you are teaching from Sunday to Sunday you may begin frequently by refreshing the class members as to where they are in the current study. If so, do it swiftly. Under certain circumstances you will need to begin by laying out a few ground rules: "Please feel free to interrupt and ask questions at any time" and that sort of thing. You will relieve audience tension, also, if you tell them *early* in the speech what material you expect to cover. A listener can check an attack of restlessness during point two if he knows he must endure only through point three. But when you indicate no limits, he envisions himself sitting through eternity while you drone away at him.

Printed material faces a stiffer challenge. It lies before the reader with all the charm of an algebraic formula. It has no bright eyes, no smiles, no new suit, nor deep resonance to assist it. Therefore it must begin pungently, with a subject of *substance* followed quickly by a verb of *substance*. Not: There were several things wrong with the church in Luther's day. But: Six abuses of power sparked the Reformation.

Whether you write or speak, keep the first sentence short; fifteen words or under, if possible.

SUMMARY

Good communication, then, begins in the mind. Sort out your precise message; tell it as one human being to another; be assured that you must win a hearing.

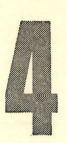 

To Produce Economy

Economy means communicating without unnecessary words. Without *any* unnecessary words. Our communication ought to exhibit the same compact trimness of a well-worked crossword puzzle: every letter fitting its place and none spilling over the sides.

To shape such material requires dungaree-thinking. We must forage the mind for phrases, test them for appropriateness, accept some, reject others. Sometimes we must cross out and begin all over again.

For this work too many Christians don slacks and a sport shirt. A typical dialogue runs like this:

> Question: What are you going to speak on?
> Answer: They've asked me to do something on Christmas.
> Question: What do they want to accomplish?
> Answer: Oh, the usual thing, I guess.
> Question: Have you written something out?
> Answer: I've got a general idea what I'm going to say—up here (pointing to head).
> Question: When do you speak?
> Answer: In a half hour.

How casual we are! As if God doled out crackerjack messages at the last minute to the careless.

We are especially nonchalant if our assignment is small. No faction in America squanders brief opportunities to get a hearing like Christians. Commissioned to write a book or conduct a week of meetings, we come through fairly well. But asked to "say a few words" on something or present a five-minute devotional, we emit disgusting, disconnected trivia. An audience would profit more by communing with God and themselves in Quaker silence than by trying to "get something" out of our remarks. Men allow us spot announcements and, because we aren't given the whole show, we skip out on rehearsals.

Yet we call "Master" one who said, "The man who is reliable in small things can be trusted with important matters . . ."[1] If Christians aren't stirring up the world—if we aren't writing the Broadway plays, the prize-winning novels, the message movies, the outstanding books—it's probably because we haven't yet learned how to compose a really decent paragraph.

How, then, shall we deal with our humbler assignments: with reports, letters, inspirational talks, short articles, and others? How shall we produce economy? First, we close the communicating vents, so that our words don't run out senseless and diffuse. Then we do four things. (1) We consider the total communicating situation. (2) We proportion our message to the time (or space) given. (3) We organize our material in *writing*. (4) We prune. Each step acts as a restricting agent forcing us to compose a pertinent, economical massage.

1. CONSIDER SITUATION

The setting or place of our presentation plays a big role in what we say and how we say it. Are we leading vespers beside a rippling lake? Have we a 4:30 A.M. TV spot launching the day's programming? Are we writing a pageant for the seniors to present at a family night? Or an article for our denomination's magazine? The situation determines, in part, our approach.

For example, if you are asked to write a Lenten meditation

for the local newspaper, you will not submit a warmed-over sermon. What you said in a hushed sanctuary on Sunday morning will not do, squeezed in between "Fire Guts Apartment" and "Two Held for Questioning." In a newspaper your material must compete with naked realism. Let your first sentence sound saccharine, and even your own church members won't finish the column.

Ordinarily, a meditation can begin with an easy, flowing sentence. But in this case, it needs to start out tersely. "Jerusalem spelled death in capital letters; but Jesus set his face to go there." Or, "Jesus told them outright: 'The Son of man will be delivered into the hands of men, and they will kill him.'"

Again, your place on a given program needs to be considered. If you are first, you can be somewhat more detailed and technical. But the later you are scheduled the simpler, livelier, and shorter you must make your comments. If you are last, you had better bring along special visual or audio effects to assist.

All that goes on at a meeting is part of it. And the audience does not make the fine distinctions between its elements that the leaders do. From the pulpit or lectern, sentences fall into categories: some are announcements, some are prayers, some are sermons. But in the pew all sentences are sentences. Their variety does not mitigate their length. Hence, if you are slated to speak for twenty minutes, and the person introducing you eats ten minutes of your time, you cannot ignore the problem. The audience braced itself for twenty minutes of courteous listening. You can't resent their restlessness if you run full time.

The setting sometimes works against us. Struggling to teach eternal truths in the church's furnace room for want of space. Mailing our appeal for funds so that it arrives with the bank's notice of an overdraft. Conducting an early morning Easter service in a driving rain.

But often it works *for* us. And we ought to let it. How many churches at resort areas disregard their advantages. Some have the Atlantic or the Pacific Ocean as their backyard. Yet never once during the season does the congregation hear:

> O LORD, how manifold are thy works!
> In wisdom hast thou made them all;
> the earth is full of thy creatures.
> Yonder is the sea, great and wide,
> which teems with things innumerable,
> living things both small and great.
> (Ps. 104:24-25.)

Mountain views that take your breath away bless other churches, yet the minister never preaches on the giving of the Ten Commandments or the Transfiguration. If churches at historic sites rush to inform us that "George Washington worshiped here," should not churches at scenic locations draw attention to the wonderful works of God? With what genuine adoration might a congregation in the right place be led in using the lines of St. Francis: "Praised be my Lord for our brother the wind, and for air and cloud, calms and all weather, by which Thou upholdest in life all creatures."[2] We need make no fewer appeals to the eye and the heart than God does.

Keep the communicating situation in mind.

2. PROPORTION THE MESSAGE

The amount of time or space given also plays a role in what we say and how we say it. Wise communicators work on the principle: The less time or space we have, the less we try to do. Which sounds lazy, but isn't. It involves three sub-principles.

(a) The less time or space given, the smaller portion of a subject we should handle.

Let us suppose you have spent three months at an ecumenical work camp, and the inevitable time has come for a "brief report." You *can* try to handle the whole subject, the whole experience. You can say: "We lived in close quarters with young people from other lands. We had to learn to understand their points of view. We had to adjust to their forms of courtesy and accept them even when they seemed strangest. We had to . . ." On and on.

Such a report covers the summer and rings true. So what? It conveys nothing but haze and blots. A person who had never been near the camp could do as well. You've snapped the picture from so far back in order to crowd everything in, that everything has slipped out of focus.

Limited by time or space, the effective communicator acts like a photographer's enlarger. He concentrates on but a section of the picture. This he "blows up" so that it appears with striking clarity. Details missed in the concentrated whole take shape. Blurs become faces and objects.

"I met Ingrid in our bunkroom and took an instant dislike to her. She wore her hems one inch below the fashion line and criticized me for chewing gum." Or, "Hans stomped into the dining hall with a Leica around his neck and a chip on his shoulder."

Ah, that's better; the work camp is coming to life. A careful recounting of how you became reconciled to Ingrid's hems and she to your gum, or of how a strong friendship developed between you and Hans, will capture the very essence of the summer. Your picture will be sharp, distinct, and interesting.

Here so many Christian communicators fail. They try to cover impossible territory.

Missionaries try to portray too much of their work in one letter. "One of our patients, Phillippe, is showing an interest in the Christian faith. He has asked for a Bible. Another one . . ." No, don't rush on; show us Phillippe. To you he is a person. To us he is nineteen vague words. Help us see him, too.

"The great gouge in Phillippe's leg is equalled only by the chasm in his soul. Clutching the New Testament, he props himself up in his bamboo bed near the doorway. He reads with his wide black eyes, his index finger, his hunched shoulders, and his unfilled heart. This morning he paused halfway down a page and looked up ponderingly. 'The good shepherd lays down his life for the sheep,' I heard him read out loud in his soft dialect."

There, Phillippe is coming into focus.

Most Bible teachers make the same mistake. They try to cover the entire Sermon on the Mount or all facets of the parable of the Prodigal Son at one sitting. How much richer their studies if they embraced less material.

Amateur writers wade into subjects like "The Decay of Family Life in Modern Times" or "Paul's Influence on Western Culture" in *essays,* not realizing that these are subjects for books —indeed, for sets of books. In lesser media we cannot do them justice.

The less time or space we are given, the smaller the truth we should handle.

(b) The less time or space we are given, the less depth we should attempt. We may enlarge one section of a big picture but must not try to give the whole picture a second or third dimension.

For example, in a brief report on your work camp experience, you won't delve into the contents of the eighty-five Bible studies you had. Or try to analyze the events of the summer in the light of Buber's I-Thou philosophy or Augustine's *City of God.*

You will not bring up matters that require elaborate background information, or ideas so basic or profound that they almost elude language. You will evade the scholars unless you can present them with the care they deserve.

Even so, you may be accused of "being deep." So accustomed is the ordinary churchgoer to banalities that he labels anything different "profound." He frequently mistakes the enlargement technique for depth. So long as you keep the distinction clear, you won't become vain. To enlarge means to tell a portion of a matter in specific detail; to "be deep" means to struggle with concepts difficult to grasp. The less time or space we have, the less depth we should handle.

(c) Finally, the less time or space given, the less we should try to do with or to our audience or readers.

Plays and movies run about two to two and one-half hours. They drive for one response: laughter, tears, suspense, or terror. They don't run the gamut.

Christian communicators need to take the hint. Our receivers are not faucets capable of dispensing hot-and-cold-running emotions at the drop of a phrase.

Back in the days when "divine services" ran all day Sunday, ministers could elicit praise, repentance, thanksgiving, fear, love, dedication, and what have you. For, by perceptive use of the various parts of the long service, they could build up sincere feelings in their congregations. But when services dropped to an hour, church fathers simply telescoped all the former elements into the new schedule. Meanwhile, people's glands still worked on the old. And still do. Any successful lover will tell you that you don't push the doorbell and, when "she" answers, poke a ring on her finger. Securing a genuine, appropriate response from a person involves sensitive preparation.

Thus, in a fifteen-minute devotional period (or less) you will not try to evoke both adoration *and* remorse. Or pity *and* gratitude. In such a brief, difficult period you will sustain one general tone throughout.

In a short report of your work camp, you will not try to project (1) your exhaustion at the end of the first week; (2) the reverence of the communion services; and (3) your eventual sense of oneness in Christ. Not in a truly brief report.

In a missionary letter you will not push for concern for Phillippe plus funds for a new maternity ward plus prayer for two lepers. Not on a single mimeographed sheet. Each of these requires an inner shifting of gears. In such a limited space you cannot give your readers the momentum to do the shifting necessary.

The less time or space we have, the less we should try to do with or to our receivers.

3. ORGANIZE MATERIAL

When a man sits down to his typewriter and begins knocking out an article without any prior plotting of what he will say, he turns out sentences like this:

> A child is first in the home, the church comes next if the child is in a Christian home, then comes the school, and after many preparatory years, at 16 to 18 years of age, there comes the college.

The same garbled mélange streams out when he speaks extemporaneously. Words with wrong connotations crop up. Sentences slide into paragraphs where they don't belong. Important matters are overlooked or receive scant treatment. A disproportionate amount of attention goes to items of little consequence, giving them a significance they do not deserve. An audience with the capacity to appreciate your message may be so confused, repulsed, or misguided by your remarks that it fails to act or does the very thing you didn't want it to do. The risk is too great.

Have you an assignment? Get a piece of paper, a pencil with a big eraser, and a place where you can concentrate. Divide the paper something like the chart on the next page.

Such a form or framework surpasses an outline, for it requires a genuine thinking-through of the material. Jotting down subjects at various indentations can be deceiving. You write:

TWO PROSPECTS FOR LIFE

I. The Life of the Flesh
    A. Opposed to the Spirit
    B. Fruits
        1. Immorality
        2. Impurity
        3. Licentiousness, etc.

II. The Life of the Spirit
    A. Opposed to the Flesh
    B. Fruits
        1. Love
        2. Joy
        3. Peace, etc.

and believe you have set out a whale of a message. But all you've done is filch the skeleton of part of a message Paul wrought out for the Galatians in A.D. 49! You haven't really figured out the relationships between I and II or A and B or among 1, 2, and 3.

And you have ignored the two catalysts of communication: the purpose and the people.

If you gave the message as outlined, what would you be try-

Purpose:		General Plan:
Part:	Intended to:	Material to do this:
Opening	Get attention and	
Body	Keep attention and	
Closing	Keep attention and	
Opening sentence*	Get attention and	
Closing sentence*		

* The opening and closing sentences are so very important you will want to give special attention to them.

ing to do? Is this, indeed, what you should be doing with your particular receivers?

What should you be doing with them? What *is* your aim?

In church school lessons, a purpose is usually furnished. Where it is, the communicator needs to ask three questions. First, is the purpose absolutely clear? Watch out for phrases like "provide Christian opportunities" or "arrive at a Christian understanding" or "secure a more Christian perspective on."

The lesson writer has thrown you a curve. He either doesn't know or prefers not to come right out and say what specific behavior or thought process he is calling for, so he uses the word "Christian" as a dodge. Where the stated purpose exhibits fuzzy thinking, rewrite it in sharp terms for your group or class.

Secondly, is it possible? Many lesson purposes sound like they were composed in Shangri-La:

> To guide young people into an appreciation of every person as worthy in the sight of God; to help them consider their own social contacts in the light of this truth so that they overcome prejudices against those who are different from them and accept all men in love.

And take the roll, too? It isn't possible. The less time we have the less we can do with or to people.

We speak of God's "unfolding purposes" and we speak wisely. If you have ever unfolded a tablecloth or a piece of paper, you know that you do it one fold at a time. Use realistic purposes, one at a time.

Thirdly, is the goal pertinent? Especially is it pertinent for the day it's to be presented? Most lessons are arranged with the age group in mind, but, because they appear in magazines or quarterlies, they cannot be current. A sudden death, the flaring of strife, or a new move in international politics can devastate them. For awesome events (and we are in for some) can so capture your class' attention that you won't be able to dislodge it. And since we hold that our faith faces and copes with life as it is, we may not *want* to dislodge it.

In *Your God Is Too Small* J. B. Phillips tells of an experiment with a class of young people. "They were asked to answer, without reflection, the question: 'Do you think God understands radar?' In nearly every case the reply was 'No,' followed of course by a laugh, as the conscious mind realized the absurdity of the answer." [3] How many irrelevant class periods had they been forced to sit through?

If headlines see man landing on the moon and you persist in trudging through "The Significance of the Inter-Testament Period on the Synoptic Gospels," you will both lose your class and pigeonhole God in an out-of-date classification.

Keep aware of what is going on in your class and in the world, so that your aims will be apt.

Oftimes no purpose is furnished. Then you must work one out in the light of God's will for your receivers. This involves prayer. It also involves a tenacious keeping-before-you of those who will hear or read you—their ages, their education, their interests, and their needs. Shape the message on the basis of all you know about them. Then you will not address young mothers on "How to Use Your Leisure Time" nor lecture juniors on quartodecimanism.

Communication, remember, does not consist in setting forth or down a message. It consists in propelling a message into the lifestream of others. Thoreau said, "It takes two to speak the truth—one to speak and one to hear." [4] It is sheer folly to expect people to rivet their minds on material that is over their heads or unrelated to their situations simply because you think it's so "good for them."

You don't need to sugarcoat or avoid unpleasant topics. But you do need to cater to a free, busy, sophisticated clientele.

Once you have a purpose, don't sabotage it. Keep every sentence, every phrase, *every word* moving toward it. When discussing something agreeable, something you want your receivers to view with favor, use terms with pleasant connotations:

> . . . give, and it will be given to you; good measure, pressed down, shaken together, running over, will be put into your lap. [5]

> The surge and thunder of the sea, the smell of wood smoke, the woods carpeted with bluebells, and a hundred other

things can touch and move our spirits in a way Science is powerless to explain.[6]

When you take up a disgusting topic, something you want your receivers to dislike, use detestable terms:

> Like a dog that returns to his vomit
> is a fool that repeats his folly.[7]

> The bottom of man's hell is a malignant relationship with God.[8]

Keep your arguments marshaled logically. Do not throw evidence for and evidence against a subject willy-nilly into the same paragraph. Avoid confusing mixtures of ideas.

A paragraph like this appeared in a recent booklet:

> The church of Jesus Christ ought to exhibit real unity and tolerance, for true Christianity abolishes barriers between men and men. Yet organized Christianity has sometimes been a chief offender. A minister in a prominent church took a second glance at the elders one morning as they passed out the communion elements. Later he exclaimed, "Where but in the church could one see such a sight: an apprentice accountant and the vice president of Universal Oil serving together."

Now *why* the sentence: "Yet organized Christianity has sometimes been a chief offender"? It does not blend with the sentence preceding it; it does not blend with what follows.

To make the statement is certainly permissible. Nor do we question its truth. But to insert it in this paragraph hinders progress. For the reader expects the minister-story to substantiate the *intolerant* nature of the organized church, and probably many readers tried so to construe it. A few, when they couldn't wrench that meaning out of it, went back to the first sentence and got the point. Others, puzzled, simply rushed on to the next paragraph or put the booklet aside as "too deep."

Organize your material.

4. PRUNE YOUR COPY

Minister to wife: "Do you think I put enough fire into my sermon?"

Wife to minister: "To tell the truth I didn't think you put enough of your sermon in the fire."

Be sure to put enough of your message in the fire. Go over it and prune away the unnecessary.

In a *short oral* devotional don't tell people you are "reading from one of my favorite passages." Let's face it, *all* devotionals are shaped around favorite passages. In telling us, you waste seven words which could be furthering the development of whatever mood or thought you desire.

Don't tell people you are reading from the King James Version of the Bible or that John Oxenham wrote the poem you are about to (or just did) read. You don't need to document a devotional.

Make no references whatsoever to the time. Especially not to its brevity. You only make a nervous audience more nervous.

Weed out such say-nothing phrases as "It is obvious that," "There was no doubt that," "I need not mention that," "There was evidence to support the fact that," etc., etc.

Don't overwork the adjective "real"; it means virtually nothing. (In a very real sense he is a real Christian having had a real experience. Good for him!)

Don't start every other sentence with "actually" or "as a matter of fact." These are TV-isms.

If you are writing a missionary letter (or any letter), don't consume the first paragraph apologizing for not writing sooner. If you have been busy, the body of the letter will disclose it.

Prune away the unnecessary.

SUMMARY

To produce economy: (1) Consider the total communicating situation; (2) proportion your message according to the time or space given; (3) organize your material; and (4) prune.

To Produce Energy

Energy means communicating with force. The Bible calls the messages of God goads that try the soul; sword-blades that pierce to the division of soul and spirit, joints and marrow. So often we make them meringue!

We write: "In many of the areas discussed we need to be aware that we are facing very real symptoms of a larger complex that is given its contemporary shape by the culture." How shall we compel men into the Kingdom with drivel?

How shall we give our messages energy? The answer is threefold. (1) We employ words of substance. (2) We work with subjects we know. (3) We keep our style simple.

1. WORDS OF SUBSTANCE

Consider the following pages. They show phrases chosen at random from two works dealing with the same subject. As your eyes fall over the words, which page beckons you to read more?

47

sunshine and rain

                            in all the close-up facts of their living

                                           clear, cool

spring of water

                          city tanks and pipes

                                           control the

rains, conquer space, and achieve any travel speed desired

                                hurling our little man-made

worlds

                                         cushioned

and padded defenses

                                bottle of bourbon

budget plans, electrical appliances, insulation[1]

Words from page 120 of *Christian Family Living*, 1958, chapter entitled "At Home With God in Your Home."

                    of such men

                         that we are

                                             that

there is no

                    If it is

          let us point out that

          is a real part

                    to provide for

                                        it is not only worth

as much but it is as genuine

                                   This cannot be

postponed

          is when that

                         ordinarily it cannot be put in[2]

Words from page 144 of *The Fine Art of Living Together*, 1927, chapter entitled "The Old Family Altar in a New Age."

Expressions of substance in the page on the left make the difference. "Is a real part" and "is when that" never leave the page. But "city tanks and pipes" and "bottle of bourbon" hoist themselves up out of print to create a mental image. J. B. Phillips tells us, ". . . they must be the right words shaped cunningly to pass men's defences and explode silently and effectually within their minds." Of course theology does not always lend itself to such terms as city tanks, but Paul related it to such unlikely matters as wrestling, racing, and donning armor. Guided by the Holy Spirit, men of God hammered out sentences of strength and substance.

A paragraph is like a rodeo. The first sentence forms a fence around the whole topic. It causes onlookers to focus their attention on a given area. As the paragraph proceeds, individual thoughts leap out into the ring one at a time to perform. In expository writing they explain the topic, give an example of it, support it, or prove it. In fiction, they carry forward the narrative. The last sentence in a paragraph may attempt a summary or prepare for the next topic or both.

The structure guides us to the level of words. Topic sentences garner the general, more vague words and rightly so. They must throw out enough ill-defined thought, enough blank area, to permit the subsequent sentences space for defining and substantiating.

Topic sentences can say:

> The church has wandered from its objective.
> Easter proclaims a mighty truth.
> The prophets cried out for social justice.

But the sentences that follow must run and jump and bob and put on a lively show or the onlookers will demand their money back.

Christians use a whole vocabulary of vacant phrases—phrases with only broad meaning. They depend upon "what follows" to give them color and vitality. Use them (if you must) sparsely and with care. When they salt and pepper your communication, your receivers are bored stiff. Check especially for these:

aim(s)	goal(s)	process(es)
approach(es)	help(s)	purpose(s)
area(s)	meaning(s)	relationship(s)
blessing(s)	objective(s)	resource(s)
concept(s)	perspective(s)	responsibility(ies)
consideration(s)	plan(s)	sin(s)
conviction(s)	preparation(s)	situation(s)
element (s)	principle(s)	term(s)
experience(s)	problem(s)	view(s)

Attaching vague adjectives to such words to form "basic plans," "particular situations," and "preliminary preparations" only makes the phrases worse.

Theologian Helmut Thielicke refreshes his communication by matching unlikely adjectives with nouns. Thus he writes of "unventilated piety," "icy desert," "domineering appeal," "pomade-slicked emptiness," "phosphorescent putrefaction," and "royal realism."[3]

In general, however, you do better to transmit meaning through your verbs. Adjectives clutter your clauses and slow down the reading rate. But verbs shuttle the mind toward your goal:

> . . . if any one strikes you on the right cheek, turn to him the other also . . .[4]

> When Adam flouted him He could have canceled Adam.[5]

> Doubt builds no cathedrals, and sings no songs . . .[6]

Adjectives not only clutter, they keep poor company. They appear so often escorted by some form of the verb "to be." And we get:

> . . . if anyone is unruly to you, do not be unruly to him.

> When Adam was unfaithful to him, God could have been unfaithful to Adam.

> Doubt is a negative attitude.

How insipid! How pitiful!

Everytime you are tempted to use "is" or "was" or "are" or "were," pause to see if there isn't some other way of projecting the subject. Sometimes you can avoid it by using a colon:

Biliousness: an affection of the liver frequently mistaken for piety.[7]

Where "to be" looks like your sole choice, test some of these:

animates	embraces	instills	shapes
appears	enfolds	involves	stays
arises	enhances	looms	substitutes
composes	enlivens	promotes	succeeds
constitutes	establishes	pulses	supports
creates	formulates	remains	undergirds
develops	generates	replaces	
displays	includes	savors	

Use "to be" when you need it to make a comparison:

True religion is betting one's life that there is a God.[8]

Love is an inward openness to the needs of others.[9]

Use it when the innate cleverness of the sentence will make up for the weak verb:

Doubts are the messages of the Living One to the honest.[10]

. . . all conduct is some philosophy gone off on an errand.[11]

Use it when you can couple it into a sentence with other stronger verbs and verb forms:

To try to forget, to laugh and drink and labor, refusing to look at what we have done, is to seal the wound and to spread the poison.[12]

If this vision you have of God does not move and drive and pull and tug and wrench and twist and hold and stride and walk off grimly after Him, it is nothing.[13]

Use it when you want to arrest speed and create a contemplative frame of mind:

The Lord is my shepherd . . .[14]

I am the resurrection and the life . . .[15]

God is in the midst of her, she shall not be moved . . .[16]

Finally, use "to be" when anything else sounds so stilted or absurd that you must.

When the time comes to speak your message, again let the verbs transmit your meaning. Hit them with a level tone of voice. Say: "For God so *loved* the world that he *gave* . . ."[17] Not: "For God so LO-Ved the world that he gA-AVe . . ."

Many Christians stress pronouns when they refer to the deity. But this expression:

> But if we *have died* with Christ, we believe that we *shall also live* with him.[18]

is stronger than:

> But if we have died with *Christ,* we believe we shall also live with *him.*

The word "this" *ruins a great deal* of communication. Amateurs write:

> This part of this section should help the committee to look at the church's life in the light of this mighty act of God and, with this in view, determine what the goals for this season will be.

Here, instead of calling our attention to something important, it takes on the emptiness of the cry "wolf, wolf." Repeated again and again it means *nothing.* Saying "this mighty act" makes the act no mightier than saying "the mighty act." Saying "this season" in no way enhances the period, although amateurs persist in thinking so.

How much more telling to write of "the Passover," "the destruction of Jericho," "the Resurrection," or whatever precisely "this mighty act" was! How much clearer to speak of Thanksgiving or Epiphany or spring or whatever "this season" is!

Reserve "this" (and "that," "these," and "those") for two special occasions: (a) when you want to distinguish between two things:

> Every one who drinks of *this* water will thirst again, but whoever drinks of the water that I shall give him will never thirst . . .[19]

(b) when you need to strain out and identify something of importance:

Mordecai to Esther: "And who knows whether you have not come to the kingdom for such a time as *this*?"[20]

Give substance and accuracy also (where you can) to words denoting number, time, and place.

Not:	*But:*
many	2000
few	5
a long time ago	in A.D. 70
in the near future	two weeks from today
from one city to another	from Corinth to Jerusalem
a certain address	the house of Judas on the street called Straight

Minimize qualifying words and phrases. Definite statements ring with energy. But a Milquetoast image emerges when you overwork: may, perhaps, tends to, could, might, seems, tries to, seeks to, strives to, and probably.

Use words of substance.

2. WORK WITH FAMILIAR SUBJECTS

Many Christian communicators begin (and end!) their careers by tackling subjects outside their ken. People who have never seen anything more gory than a scratched finger want to write the stoning of Stephen or the death of Savonarola. The landlocked want to recount Paul's shipwreck, while the well want to portray Naaman the leper.

Inevitably such efforts fail. We cannot write or speak convincingly of things we haven't experienced. Our accounts lack the necessary details, accuracy, and impact. Take Phillippe on page 37 as an example. He is a figment of the author's imagination. I have never been abroad.

As a portrait of a man reading eagerly, the words have reality, for I have seen a man absorbed in a book. But the rest is very questionable. To make Phillippe sound like a native at a mission station, I gave him "black eyes," "a bamboo bed," and a "soft dialect." But natives with black eyes may speak in piercing dialects. And bamboo may abound in countries where people have brown eyes. Indeed it may have properties that make it highly unsuitable for use in beds. I don't know.

Bona fide missionaries and world travelers, however, will know and will probably get a chuckle over Phillippe. To them, I'm sure, the account sounds shaky and make-believe. Were it longer, it would appear increasingly absurd, even to stay-at-homes.

Many sections of Scripture are virtually "off limits" to Americans. We have never starved; how can we depict the sieges of the Old Testament? We have never known national defeat; how can we appreciate Lamentations? We have never been a vassal people; how can we understand ". . . render to Caesar the things that are Caesar's, and to God the things that are God's"?[21]

Without generous quantities of imagination, empathy, and research, we can't. Serious communicators live with their material before they attempt to convey it to others. Listen to this blurb about Leon Uris:

> Among the marks of this young ex-Marine's devotion to his craft is the painstaking research that precedes the actual writing of his novels. For *Exodus* he visited many countries of Europe, traveled more than 12,000 miles within the borders of tiny Israel alone, then spent a year building a novel out of the material he had unearthed. . . . So it was with *Mila 18.* As Quentin Reynolds points out elsewhere in this announcement, Uris steeped himself for months in the pitiful reminders of brutality—and heroism—which still haunt the scene of the crime in Warsaw or linger ineradicably in the minds of the few who survived that disaster. Then he began to write.[22]

If you have an assignment and obtaining firsthand experience is impossible, get secondhand experience. Can you find something written by a person who faced the situation in your assignment? Read it. Can you find a picture or pictures of people in the situation (in popular magazines that depict the news perhaps). Study them.

Become as familiar with your subject as you can.

Long, complicated sentences bog the reader down, exhaust the listener's attention.* Norman Shidle warns that they should ". . . enter everyday writing only when put there by design; only when the writer consciously decides for slow pacing. Most long-sentence writing is not so born. Usually, it results from . . . the writer's inability to do any better."[23]

See the difference:

To illustrate, the big problem with atomic energy is not whether men can learn how to explode larger bombs, but whether men can be developed with moral trustworthiness and discerning insight to know how, why and when such great force should be employed and how to adapt this energy to useful ends. (52 words)	Yes, they all attempt bridge-heads, but just as it is impossible to build a bridge across a chasm without starting from both sides, so it proves impossible in this matter of a moral gulf to do more than erect a painful and desperate bridgehead, *unless Someone is also building from the other side.*[24] (53 words)

The long sentence on the left proceeded from the writer's inability to do any better (at least at the moment). Dealing with powerful, life-and-death issues, it should have displayed a terse pithiness:

> To illustrate, atomic power confronts mankind with an agonizing question. Not, can we teach men to explode larger bombs? But, can we invest them with such insight and integrity that they will use the energy for constructive ends?

Instead the writer drained away all impetus by his meandering clauses.

The sentence on the right was "put there by design." It concerns the great gulf between God and man and the futility of man's trying to build a bridge across it. All this the long sentence reflects. As one word gives way to another, then an-

---

* However, sentences in speeches can be somewhat longer than written sentences.

other, the gap yawns wider and wider and the prospect of bridging it, slimmer and slimmer.

To write in a simple style, you must keep "above" your material. Not "above" in the aloof sense that the nineteenth-century writers were. But "above" in the sense that you dominate the words, the words do not dominate you.

You are like a professional mountain climber, experiencing all the hardships, hazards, and thrills of your customers, save one: *You know the path.*

To avoid enmeshment requires a particular thinking-sequence. You conceive the main subject, main verb, and main object (where there is one) in every sentence before you write it. You produce the independent clause before going on to any dependent clauses.

Newspapers are easy to read because journalists train their minds this way. While uncasing their typewriters, they are composing mentally "man bites dog" or "gunman eludes police." Main subject. Main verb. Main object. The trimmings (like: "Despite an extensive roadblock, the gunman eluded the police") are added afterward.

Not so with amateur communicators. They write clause at a time as it comes, whether the thought be dependent or independent. You see it in the atomic-energy sentence. The writer's thought began with "To illustrate..." Had he spotted "developed" as one of his main verbs before he started, he wouldn't have linked "with" to it. Men are not developed "with" moral trustworthiness or discerning insight. Normal English usage calls for "into."

A clear, simple style will emerge if you discipline yourself to think:

> God created the world . . .
> God sent his Son . . .
> Christ called disciples . . .
> the Spirit helps our infirmities . . .

Add link words (but, therefore, because, and others), adjectives, adverbs, and dependent clauses later.

"Have's" and "has's" also complicate your style and dissipate energy:

> We have generally taken it for granted that we shall have a Sunday school, and we have spent a great deal of money building it up.

But if you (a) use present tense (or the simple past) wherever possible and (b) use active rather than passive voice, you lick the problem.

Life magazine recently reviewed the play *A Man for All Seasons*. If ever an account had an excuse for using the past tense, this one did: The play had already been performed and it told the story of Thomas More, who lived back in 1529! But see how much the critic, by his shrewd manipulation of time, cast in the present:

> Most playwrights have a pretty low opinion of modern man, who *appears* all too often on the stage as a futile, lost soul. So it *is* heartening to *behold* such a specimen of humanity as Sir Thomas More, whose wit and vigorous integrity *shine* through Broadway's hit, *A Man for All Seasons*.
>
> The play, by Englishman Robert Bolt, *takes up* More as England's chancellor in 1529 when he began to *lock horns* with Henry VIII. Ordered to *sanction* the king's divorce from Catherine of Aragon so he *can wed* Anne Boleyn, More *remains* loyal to the Church of Rome and *refuses to grant* that a king, *be* he ever so mighty, *can flout* God's laws. Sir Thomas *is acted* with strong, forthright modesty by England's Paul Scofield and the play *is* free of the stilted rigamarole of most historical drama. Between them, star and playwright *bring* stature to the modern theater as they *sweep* the play briskly and movingly to a proud, tragic end.[25]

When the context forces no particular tense upon you, use the present. Dr. Buttrick might have said:

> Doubt has built no cathedrals nor has it sung songs of praise.

But how much more vivid:

> Doubt builds no cathedrals and sings no songs.

Passive voice sounds equally listless:

No cathedrals have been built and no songs of praise have been sung as a result of doubt.

Thus, when you check over a page, if it looks choked with "have's" and "has's," try switching some of the objects into subjects. Change:

Many miracles have been recorded in the Bible.

to:

The Bible records many miracles.

Several other procedures contribute to a simple style: (a) keeping antecedents clear; (b) maintaining consistency in person, number, and tense; (c) keeping phrases and clauses parallel.

When your reader has to back up and re-read several sentences to get the gist of what you're saying and even then isn't altogether sure, he loses the sense of energy you build up. Take this example:

Peter denied his Lord and Judas betrayed him. Afterwards he went out and hanged himself. (Who did?)

When you use a pronoun, be sure the reader will know the exact noun for which it stands. Place the pronoun as near its parent-noun as possible. Occasionally you will run it before:

There HE stood, a FRIEND of the accused, warming his hands over the enemy's fire.

But normally it runs after the noun:

As the soldiers grouped around the fire, PETER joined them. HE extended his fingers above the flames.

Avoid, as much as possible, pronoun expressions that have no antecedents like: "it is clear that," "there was reason to believe," etc.

Maintain consistency. Singular nouns require singular pronouns and singular verbs. Plural nouns require plural pronouns and verbs. Inconsistency brings confusion:

The group thought its work was over after they had passed the resolution.

40377

Is the "they" a mistake referring to "the group"? Or does the "they" refer to a second group that passed a resolution and put the first group out of business?

Parallelism also prevents confusion. Thoughts emerge in clean lines that are easy to follow. Awkwardness sets in when you mix active and passive voices in one sentence:

> The Spirit guides us into truth and the things that are to come are declared by him.

instead of:

> The Spirit guides us into truth and declares the things that are to come.

When you prepare your readers for a series of particular verb forms and then switch them without warning, you hinder the reader:

> The crowds welcomed Jesus in three ways. By taking off their garments and strewing them in the way. They tore down palm branches and waved them. And by singing "Hosanna to the Son of David!"

The passage reads more rapidly and energetically when the three verb forms are the same: By taking off, *by tearing down,* and by singing.

Amateurs often violate parallelism in making long lists. Run the outline like this:

> They contributed to the project:
> (a) by praying
> (b) by studying
> (c) by giving

or

> They decided:
> (a) to pray
> (b) to study
> (c) to give

> that the project might go forward.

But do not mix the forms by having some phrases begin "by praying" while others begin "to study."

Write in short, clear sentences.

SUMMARY

To produce energy: (1) Employ words of substance; (2) write and speak of things you know; (3) keep your style simple.

To Produce Subtlety

Subtlety means communicating without overdrawing conclusions for the reader. It means practicing a hard-to-define restraint. Charles Jehlinger, one-time director of the American Academy of Dramatic Arts, used to instruct apprentice actors, "Mean more than you say."[1] His advice applies not just to acting but to writing and speaking as well. *Mean* more than you say.

So many Christians say all. They do not see that modern communication is like celery. It is easy to grasp (no forks necessary), but he who takes it must chew it up himself. Teachers say, "You ought to respond to God's love for you." Or, "Don't be proud." Or, "Give to the needy." These sentences reek with truth, but have all the appeal of pre-masticated celery.

Jesus sketched God as a father scanning the horizon for sight of his wandering, wastrel son; then he left to his audience what they would do about such a One. He pictured a guest who snatched the place of honor at a feast and had to be asked to occupy a seat of less distinction when a more eminent man showed up. And thus prepared his audience for ". . . every one

63

who exalts himself will be humbled."[2] Jesus compared giving to depositing funds in a foolproof treasury. Little wonder that his sermons attracted crowds and were remembered.

But how do we produce this quality of subtlety? Like energy, it involves three practices. (1) We work with raw materials. (2) We label subordinate matters. (3) We moralize with great care.

1. WORK WITH RAW MATERIALS

Celery at its best is served raw. So is modern writing. It is as concrete, specific, and close to life as possible. Recall the two reports of work camp experiences:

We lived in close quarters with young people from other lands. We had to learn to understand their points of view. We had to adjust to their forms of courtesy and accept them even when they seemed strangest. We had to . . .	I met Ingrid in our bunkroom and took an instant dislike to her. She wore her hems one inch below the fashion line and criticized me for chewing gum.

The account on the left has been plucked, boiled until flavorless, then canned for consumption. The account on the right arrives plucked but unprocessed. It retains all the pulp and juices of the original experience.

Albert Walker in *Minimum Essentials for Good Writing* says: "Any writing which is to get the real interest of the people who read must touch in some way the subjective side of experience. By the subjective element in writing we mean (1) primarily any report or description of real experience, real interests, thoughts, attitudes, hopes and fears; or (2) facts which touch these things in people's minds."[3]

We have a powerful example of this statement in modern history. Following World War II, the German people were told that, by supporting Hitler, they had accrued responsibility for the slaughter of six million Jews. They were told this, not once, but many times and in many ways. They saw pictures of concentration camps with their starved, gaunt prisoners. They juggled embarrassing questions about why they had raised no protest to their government's brutality. But nothing happened.

Goebbels, the propaganda minister, had implanted the idea that the Jews were subhuman (they certainly looked subhuman in the concentration camp pictures) and who gets upset over the death of beasts, even six million beasts?

Then one day the play telling the story of Anne Frank penetrated the Rhineland. Repentance and shame broke out like an epidemic. Why? Because Anne's diary touched the subjective side of experience.

Six million Jews was a conclusion. It was a cold, objective figure suitable for a report regarding animals. The Germans could shrug it off.

But the diary was something else again. It blazed the raw experience of existing in constant terror across the consciences of those responsible. Here were real thoughts, real attitudes, real hopes, real fears, put down in candid truth. Back of the words pulsed no animal, but a defenseless, life-loving thirteen-year-old. No one could shrug her off.

Have you a message? Try to incarnate it. Tell it in terms of a person or people. Or in terms of objects and happenings common to the majority of your receivers. In this book certain aspects of communication are compared to baiting a hook, to a rodeo, and to celery, on the theory that most readers will know enough about these subjects to get the point. They could have been told in more remote, academic language. The Kingdom of heaven could have been compared to less subjective items than a great catch of fish, a grain of mustard seed, or a pearl. But would anyone have paid attention?

Incarnation offers all kinds of possibilities. It leaps to the side of audience participation methods. During discussion periods, people can express their interests, thoughts, attitudes, hopes, and fears. If a speaker has ventured into subjective elements unknown to his audience, a question period can bring clarity. Role-playing, rhythmic movement, play-reading and the other many creative techniques of group communication deal with the raw material of experience.

Suppose your assignment is to encourage Bible study. You have your purpose; you are casting about for a general plan.

Purpose: to encourage Bible study.	General Plan:

The Bible, your audience, the experiences of others as gleaned from interviews, books, and magazines—all contain possibilities.

You might shape a lively discussion around Matthew 4:4: "Man shall not live by bread alone, but by every word that proceeds from the mouth of God." What does it mean "to live"? Why is "bread alone" inadequate? What contribution do the words that proceed from the mouth of God make? This could lead into a study of what the words meant in their original Old Testament setting, Deuteronomy 8:3, and in their New Testament setting in Matthew.

You might take a negative approach and explore what absence of the ministry of the Word of God means in a life. Gamaliel Bradford, a prominent biographer, wrote in his journal: "I do not dare to read the New Testament for fear of its awakening a storm of anxiety and self reproach and doubt and dread of having taken the wrong path, of having been traitor to the plain and simple God. Not that I do not know perfectly well that no reading would make me believe any more. But, oh, what agonies of fret and worry it would give me; for I should be able neither to believe nor to disbelieve nor to let it alone."[4]

A three-point talk or analysis could be fashioned about Bradford's fear: (1) his fear of reading the Word; (2) his fear that his life had been lived in error; and (3) his fear that the Word might cling.

Then again, you might take the positive approach. Charles

H. Spurgeon, a well-known English minister, wrote: "I rest in the eternal fact that God hath revealed himself in Jesus as blotting out the sin of all his believing people, and, as a believer, I have the word of God as my guarantee of forgiveness. This is my rest. Because I am a believer in Christ Jesus, therefore have I hope, therefore have I joy and peace, since God hath declared that 'he that believeth in him hath everlasting life.' " [5]

Spurgeon's confident attitudes about his life, his joy, and his peace would lend themselves to treatment.

Oftimes when your point is so delicate that you fear your receivers won't "get it," you can resort to contrast. Jesus used it often. He told the story of two men who went up to pray, one self-righteous, the other meek. He included in the story of the Good Samaritan a priest and a Levite who "passed by on the other side." He contrasted the men who built their houses on sand and on rock, the wise and the foolish virgins, the sheep and the goats. His wise juxtapositions made long harangues unnecessary.

Sometimes, when you use visual aids, you can actually place the two thoughts to be contrasted side by side. On one side of a blackboard or poster you can letter "Life without the Bible" and, on the other side, "Life with the Bible." The contrast is easier to see this way than when the ideas are run in sequence:

Life without the Bible	Life with the Bible
Fearful	Peaceful
Shallow	Deep
Joyless	Joyful

2. LABEL SUBORDINATE MATTERS

But for Mark 3:19 (and other elements), Mark might have been a whodunit. Mark 3 introduces the disciples, and 3:19 reads, ". . . and Judas Iscariot, who betrayed him." In the third chapter of a sixteen-chapter book, the author gives away the whole betrayal plot. He does so because it is trivial and incidental. Mark's concern centers not on who sold out Christ to his enemies, but on what, indeed, is the meaning of the life and the death of Christ. Thus, by labeling the traitor, he destroys a minor plot which might compete with the true one, and keeps his readers probing for his real concern.

Life is too complicated to deal with *all* raw material. Out of the maze of things to be told we must select one truth toward which we push our receivers with some vivid account. Many Christians hustle after so many truths that they have time or space only for labeling. Even worse, others grow finicky about the labeling material itself. They feel that here and there the labels require qualification. Zealous to be ultra-accurate, they explain so much minutiae that their readers lose the thread of thought (not to mention their patience).* The work becomes a boring jumble instead of a swift communiqué or a clarifying study.

You can't tell everything. Whatever you say you must leave something unsaid. Take the risk; relinquish side issues in order to get to your goal.

Consider these two parables:

> [The lawyer] said to Jesus, "And who is my neighbor?" Jesus replied, "A man was going down from Jerusalem to Jericho, and he fell among robbers, who stripped him and beat him, and departed, leaving him half-dead. . . . But a Samaritan, as he journeyed, came to where he was; and when he saw him, he had compassion, and went to him and bound up his wounds, pouring on oil and wine; then he set him on his own beast and brought him to an inn, and took care of him. . . . Which of these three, do you think, proved neighbor to the man who fell among the robbers?" [6]

> "Or what woman, having ten silver coins, if she loses one coin, does not light a lamp and sweep the house and seek diligently until she finds it? And when she has found it, she calls together her friends and neighbors, saying, 'Rejoice with me, for I have found the coin which I had lost.' Even so, I tell you, there is joy before the angels of God over . . ." [7]

Note that in the Samaritan account in which the issue is "neighborliness," Jesus studiously avoids labeling anyone a neighbor. He deals, rather, with the raw materials of neighborli-

---

* See criticism of Dreiser on page 11.

ness, saying: ". . . he had compassion, and went to him and bound up his wounds, pouring on oil and wine . . ." etc.

But in the second parable, Jesus readily identifies those whom the woman calls together "friends and neighbors." Here the issue concerns lost things. To quibble over whether or not the people called together really *were* neighbors (since they weren't helping her look for her coin) is ridiculous.

Label subordinate matters.

3. MORALIZE WITH CARE

"The nervous, defensive style, the declamatory justification, do not sound as convincing as facts put in a deprecatory manner," Han Suyin told her Communist guide. And she was right. Ordinarily the facts set down selectively and without sentimentality tell the story. Ordinarily communicators need not moralize.

When the occasion arises, it must be done with care. In *Marco Millions*, Eugene O'Neill pointed his finger with considerable novelty. The play depicts Marco Polo as a shallow, greedy businessman out for the "fast buck." An epilogue ends each performance. It plants the costumed Polo on a front-row seat in the audience. As the lights come on, he blinks and looks disturbed. But by the time he has reached the lobby, he is laughing and jovial again, the play and its rebuke forgotten.

In the well-known *Screwtape Letters*, C. S. Lewis moralizes *in reverse* by presenting his readers with the directives of Satan.

In all exhortations two cautions are important. (1) Sermonize out of raw material. If you begin with reproach or admonition, don't expect an audience. Americans are too free to listen to (or read) your "oughts." Lure attention and build evidence in the beginning and the body of your message. Then spin your point out of that evidence at the end.

How can a popular secular writer like Antoine de Saint Exupéry get away with such a sermonic sentence as: "To set man free it is enough that we help one another to realize that there does exist a goal towards which all mankind is striving"?[8] First, because it is on page 236 of a 245-page book. Secondly, because the 235 pages preceding it contain raw materials to ease us up to it. As an outcome sentence, it holds up well; as an opening line, it wouldn't stand a chance.

(2) Sermonize as one human being to another. The "gifts" in *Gift from the Sea* are really lessons or morals. What helped make the book a best seller was the author's attitude: Anne Morrow Lindbergh identified herself with her readers. Remember what the blurb on the jacket said? "She does this without the overtones of preaching, but herself as a seeker, echoing—only clearer and stronger—our own small still voice."

Moralize with care.

CONCLUSION

At this point the shrewd reader is saying, "This author is simply telling me the same things over and over again in different ways." In a sense, the reader is right. The qualities "economy," "energy," and "subtlety" can be distinguished in modern communication. But the techniques for producing them blend together almost inextricably. What produces economy also produces energy and subtlety; what produces energy also produces economy and subtlety, etc., etc. You will see it even more clearly in the examples that follow.

Examples

The reader has seen a sentence or two of material illustrating facets of economy, energy, and subtlety. Let him now look at longer passages combining the qualities.

Three are examples of the typical *ingredients* in Christian messages: the recounting of a Bible narrative, the description of a religious experience, and the explaining of a doctrine.

Three are samples of *types* of messages: a missionary letter, a sermonette for a newspaper, and a short devotional.

RECOUNTING OF BIBLE NARRATIVE (1 Samuel 26:7-11)

Like a flash of forked lightning the thought tore through his mind: This is the enemy, and God has laid him here before me. God has walled him about with wagons, and stopped the ears of the host with a deep sleep. No cry would waken them, even if there were to be a cry. This is the enemy who strangled me and hurled me down to grovel and weep. This is the enemy—and not my enemy alone—enemy of Samuel and of Judah, canker in the bowels of Israel, madman upon the throne. . . . And suddenly he felt the presence of the God of hosts, the great body of the Warrior, covered with dragon scales and blowing the hot breath of the bull. The God of Battles was with him, panting for blood.

"Come now, let me smite him," said Abishai. "I pray you, let me smite him to the earth with one stroke, and there will be no need to strike him a second time."

With one stroke—God, God, David thought, what things might be accomplished with one thrust of the spear! One stroke, and I am avenged and Israel is cleansed and Jonathan is on the throne. A nameless murderer lays Saul low by night and flees; and David is recalled to live in a high house of stone and cedarwood, to walk with the great, to sing again in a green garden, to turn Israel into Caphtor, to wear a double crown. . . .

Saul stirred in his sleep. The loose lips closed and were indented briefly at the corners by a faint and transitory smile. Such a smile had transformed his face on many a sun-reddened evening in the garden at Gibeah . . . Such a smile, solemn and tender, he had bestowed a hundred times upon his lutist at the end of a song. With such a smile he had risen from the council table or walked across the field of battle to greet a hero, to welcome Abner, to embrace Jonathan. So he had smiled long ago in the tent at Ephes-Dammim, when he fell silent after telling how the men of Jabesh-Gilead had brought him their sour wine and washed his feet with their tears.

"My lord," said Abishai.

David made his shoulders hard and high against the son of Zeruiah and lifted his eyes to the stars. Jahveh still hovered between him and the firmament. But He was no longer the God of Battles—He was the Other Jahveh now, formless and all-pervading. Weep, son of Jesse, said the Lord. Weep for the hero of Jabesh-Gilead and Michmash and Amalek. Weep for him who lifted up the tribes of Israel and joined them together. Weep for this broken tabernacle in which I dwelt, for it was fair and clean and high, and I dwelt comfortably there. Cease for one moment to be David of Bethlehem. Cast off the fair flesh that stands between you and Me, and between you and all men. Put by your too-well-beloved self, and creep bodiless and self-less into that which lies before you. And if this is impossible, if you are still imprisoned in yourself even at such an hour, then weep for yourself. For you also are anointed. You also in your day will become the ravaged temple through which the sounding wind of glory and the devouring fire of shame have passed. . . .

The voice of the world, speaking in Abishai's mouth, said yet once more, "Let me lay him low, my lord."

But David turned and smiled at Abishai and shook his head. "Destroy him not," he said.[1]

Check back over the account, noticing the following:

• Use of strong, colorful verbs and verb-forms: tore, hurled, blowing, panting, smite, stirred, embrace, hovered, creep, and weep.
• Use of dialogue.
• Shift into present tense in third paragraph; partial present tense in sixth paragraph.
• Apt descriptions: "David made his shoulders hard and high against the son of Zeruiah. . ."; "Put by your too-well-beloved self, and creep bodiless and selfless into that which lies before you."
• Buttressing of forms of the verb "to be" with livelier verbs in the same sentence.
• A sense of restraint running through the whole account.

DESCRIPTION OF A RELIGIOUS EXPERIENCE

Light from the street lamp, beating through the colored glass of St. Basil's Greek Catholic Church, slanted a plum-colored glow over the priest's face, over the uplifted rows of heads before him, and ended in dark shadows under the choir loft. It was the time of evening service. Everything was quiet; the place seemed at peace. Heads turned slowly to watch Anna Kajak walk up the narrow aisle to kiss the feet of the Lord

Jesus. On the white pine floor her wet shoes left muddy marks, heel and toe, like exclamation points. Heads, turning, watched her cross at the front of the church and go down the aisle by the wall into the shadows of the back. There was almost no movement in the church. Stolid peasant hands, thick-jointed and chapped, lay on black satin laps or turned the leaves of the prayer book. Bright bows on little girls in the front pews ducked from side to side, and they stayed stiff and quiet. The men were seated in tight rows, their heads half-bowed in attitudes of respect and interest. The priest came before the altar. He took up the big gold Bible and held it before him and the little boys and girls stumbled out bashfully and kissed one of the four holy pictures on its raised cover. Then he placed the Bible on the altar. He turned toward the congregation, holding high, now, a small gold cup in which were the wine and the bread. The wine was the blood of Jesus; the bread was His flesh. While the choir was chanting the prayer, the priest ate and drank. Then he put the plate and cup back on the altar. As the priest had been drinking from the cup, the bells in the tower had clanged out even peals, which clashed against the walls and roof and broke into a million dings and dongs, and the choir had sung "Hristos Voskres's" to the pealing of the bells. The priest closed the door of the tabernacle on the golden cup. The choir finished its chants. The bells stopped. For a moment the quiet was absolute, and in the quiet a sense of peace rounded off the jagged edges of earlier sounds. Then a baby woke and began to cry. The mother nursed it, her eyes wet and gleaming as she watched the priest swing the *cadelnicha* in an arch of smoking incense. He turned slowly, swung the censer toward the mother and child. She crossed herself above the baby.[2]

Notice the following:

• Total use of the raw materials of the experience to create the mood and tone. No out-and-out statement that the evening service at St. Basil's is reverent.
• The sentences are short and uncomplicated.

• The verb "to be" is used skillfully to create the meditative scene the writer wants to depict. Nevertheless, the account is not without livelier verbs: slanted, ducked, stumbled out, clanged out, clashed, broke, rounded off, and swing.

• Apt descriptions: "slanted a plum-colored glow," "her wet shoes left muddy marks, heel and toe, like exclamation points," "stolid peasant hands, thick-jointed and chapped," "the men were seated in tight rows," "a sense of peace rounded off the jagged edges of earlier sounds."

• The word "this" does not appear in the whole account. The writer says: "Then he put the plate and cup back on the altar," resisting the temptation to call them "this plate" or "this cup."

EXPLANATION OF DOCTRINE*

The kingdom isn't some dilapidated subdivision
of the universe,
>   not some humanitarian development.
>   The world will not be perfect.
>   We have fluorescent bulbs; the heart
>   is dark with sorrow.
>   So, we have released the smallest
>   element of life, but we have sent it,
>   concentrated, into war.
>   We understand the workings of the
>   human mind, and yet the mental
>   institutions bulge with sufferers from
>   "man's own inhumanity to man."
> An English paper put it well by saying:
> "Man has conquered in the air, only to be
> compelled to burrow underground."
So many people are deceived by progress.

---

* From the book *Thine the Glory* by Wyn Blair Sutphin. Copyright, ©, 1962 by Wyn Blair Sutphin. Reprinted by permission of E. P. Dutton & Co., Inc.

Never mind that Emerson once called it all,
"Improved means to unimproved ends." Mankind is "on the up and up."
His monuments span the rivers, cross the continents, and pierce the skies.

But I do not believe in them.

A snowflake is a monument to winter, but it melts away.
A teardrop is a monument to sorrow, but it dries.
The thunder is a monument to summer, but it rolls away.

And so does progress.

It is all illusion and a breath can shatter it.

So many have obscured "the kingdom" by their private causes.

They have called it:
"Civic betterment, or
forty-hour week, or
social justice."

"God the Father, Son, and Holy Ghost," was
rapidly replaced by a new Trinity entitled, "Food,
Clothing, and Shelter," and the new utensils of
the faith became:

The broom that makes a clean sweep,
and the soap-box that harangues the
multitudes; the survey that amasses
cold statistics, and the commissions
that interpret them, so that they
are incomprehensible!

Ah, but "the Kingdom," that
elusive glory, still escapes
them, for the kingdom is:

Within, and not without.

It isn't some external circumstance, but an internal conviction.

How does God, then, change the world? By changing *you!*

His monuments are men!
Remember Jesus Christ Himself. Now, how did he attack
the world?

> You do not find Him jockeying for favorable
> appointments.
> He was never precinct leader for the party.
> Though He saw men hungry and oppressed, He
> didn't set up bread lines.

Yes, He was concerned, but no, He never treated the
externals; He got down to souls!

> He knew that power never changes nature, only
> places.

>> It can only be transferred, but not
>> transformed.
>> What matter whether it be medieval
>> despotism, or modern dictatorship?

You see, the point is this:

>> "No rearrangement of bad eggs can make a
>> satisfactory omelet!"
>> It is the heart of man that counts!

What, after all, is history? Is it the cold, impartial
record of events, or is it heated by the warm biographies
of men?

>> Who can recall the party ticket Lincoln ran
>> upon? or
>> Who can name the war when Florence Night-
>> ingale began her work?
>> I tell you, history is men!

Notice:

● Use of household words: fluorescent bulbs, snowflake, broom,
soap-box, bread lines, omelet.
● Strong verbs: bulge, span, pierce, shatter, amasses, escapes,
attack, heated.
● In the sixty-two clauses containing verbs, forty-one are cast
in the present or future tenses; twenty-one in the past.
● Short sentences.

- Injection of questions and exclamatory sentences to vary the pace and break up the monotony of declaratives.
- Good use of contrast: "We have fluorescent bulbs; the heart is dark with sorrow." "We understand the workings of the human mind, and yet the mental institutions bulge with sufferers ..."
- "This" occurs only once.

A MISSIONARY LETTER

While we vacationed at Kihindo rest house, war broke out in Bukavu between Lumumba's and Mobutu's men. We followed each newscast and inter-mission communication two or three times a day. On January 6, Goma police confiscated the Goma and Kihindo transmitters and those stations had no further contact with other stations or the outside—"ham" operators in Uganda and Ruanda were assisting. We cut short the "rest," went back to Singa and packed two drums of books, tools, etc. to store in Uganda until calm ...

Not wishing to leave the family alone, we journeyed to Ruanguba (Ellen and Elfreida already there), just 10 miles from the Uganda border. After taking drums and (hidden) guns across, deteriorating news sent Don back to Singa (100 miles interior) to pack clothing. On January 13 he took the family to Kirwa wolfram mines, British side. With news of war in Goma, he and Charles Trout returned to help some of the single women, still at Ruanguba, to leave Congo.

Though the local commandant had agreed to the plan in the afternoon, soldiers turned back the first three cars (Don and five girls) at the border that evening, menacing with their guns and pulling Don's nose a bit. No Europeans would pass, they said. The other Ruanguba personnel were following, since news of increasing atrocities had led faithful Africans to advise their missionaries to leave. They were turned back short of the border. Back again at Ruanguba, the soldiers declared Don was a Belgian, not a missionary, and should be taken to their camp for "treatment." Eventually, a Christian among them persuaded his buddies that Don was a missionary, and five guards were left to keep all under "station arrest." Due to jealousy among them, two threatened to kill each other the next day, and the five were removed. That day the Pelletiers were allowed to evacuate Elfreida, 11 days post-operative, after the commander examined her at 2 A.M. to be sure she was really sick! Others got out by two's and three's during the following week.

January 19, those remaining at Ruanguba PRAYed to be released "before dark." Dr. Tom Humphrey approached the Congo border at 4 P.M., offering to go into the hospital, if all at Ruanguba were released. Advised of the meeting late, Don and the four remaining girls arrived at the border just after soldiers had told Tom he was an unwanted foreigner, and he had gone back. Pat Person told the soldiers that the commander had sent them to talk with the doctor—would they open the barrier so they could catch him? The soldiers debated, and agreed! Freedom! When Charles arrived with the commander, the latter said, "It is God's will!" and agreed for Charles to leave, too!

With all out of Ruanguba, some northern and southern missionaries were still detained in Congo. Two had been jailed, five cars confiscated, ridiculous fines imposed, property appropriated. All CBers* were released (by UN troops) by January 25. The majority of us are here in Kampala. Many have reservations to fly home. Several will proceed to our Ivory Coast field, some will investigate a new field in Senegal, some will remain in Uganda to complete translation work and maintain border contact with Congo for a while. As mission legal representative, Don may remain to do final honors for the MBK.[3]

Note:

• Don is the writer's husband. Consider, then, the restraint with which the account is told. No conclusions, just the raw materials

---

* Conservative Baptists

of the situation. We sense the confusion and fear and courage back of the words themselves.

• The verbs and verb forms are strong and express the urgency and air of crisis: broke out, cut short, menacing, pulling, threatened, evacuate, detained, confiscated, and imposed.

• The key quotation is direct: "It is God's will!"

• Dates, place names, even times of the day and night are given specifically.

SERMONETTE FOR A NEWSPAPER

God calls us into life—not away from it.

Jim Jackson got such a call. One evening the newspaper headlines shouted TEEN-AGERS CAUGHT IN BURGLARY RING. When youngsters from his own neighborhood had been arrested for speeding, the police investigation discovered the youth had been playing with some serious crime for the last several months by stealing tires, hub caps, and automobile parts. Their illicit loot totaled over $1,000.

The next day, Don Davis next door put his house up for sale and planned to move his family to a "better neighborhood."

Although the Jackson's teen-age son and daughter were not involved, Jim knew he had an obligation. He too moved swiftly. Within a week he got several neighborhood fathers to join him in forming a hot rod club for their boys to spend their desire for adventure with proper supervision. And in another week he had contacted his business friends to hire some of the boys for after-school and summer jobs to help the youth learn responsibility.

Jim didn't move away. He didn't piously condemn the youth. He got busy in helping!

I have another friend who practices medicine in a mud and thatch "hospital" in the Far East. Why should he spend his life in a place so primitive and so remote? Why should he feel any obligation to people so different from his own kind?

"When a young mother here looks at her new-born baby,

WORDS ON TARGET

she knows that he will probably die in infancy. Until recently people here treated someone with appendicitis by beating him with sticks to drive out the evil spirits.

"I didn't want to come here, but somebody had to," he says.

Jesus put it this way: "Let [a man] deny himself and take up his cross and follow me. For whoever would save his life will lose it, and whoever loses his life for my sake will find it." (Matt. 16:24b-25 RSV)

God does not need any spiritual hermits; He wants serious workers who willingly flex their muscles and pitch in when they see a job to be done.

After all, the principal purpose of life is to prepare for heaven. God wants those souls who understand holiness, righteousness, and love as living realities for eternal fellowship.

We can see that easily enough. We choose friends who appreciate the same things we do, who have the same scale of values, and who enjoy being with us. We couldn't find much satisfaction in visiting with someone who did not understand (and who refused to learn) our English language, or who ate beetles for dessert, or who hated babies.

The man who serves God with his muscles and his time as well as with his lips is preparing for heaven. He is living life, not just watching.

Not only are we to prepare ourselves for heaven, but we have an obligation to set this world in order.

Look at it this way—if a friend permitted us to use his house rent-free for a few years, we would certainly want to keep it in good repair. We would reply to his generosity by fixing a leaking roof, mowing the lawn, or painting dirty walls.

The problems of war, hatred, immorality, etc. demand our attention while we are God's guests in life. Leaving these problems for someone else to solve is sheer irresponsibility. And if we don't treat this house right, how could we expect to be invited to an even finer mansion?

Basically, all of us know that God has put in us some special talent, or interest, or concern, or ability that we must share with the world. In a sense, He has made an investment in us.

God wants the workman, not the observer. God calls us into life—not away from it.[4]

Note:

- The opening sentence is short, terse. Since a newspaper is full of the things that go on in life, accidents, thefts, rescues, and whatnot, the thought "God calls us into life" is apt.
- The writer incarnates his points, telling them in terms of people, either real or imaginary.
- Quotations are direct.
- Phrases like "flex their muscles," "pitch in when they see a job to be done," "set this world in order," "fixing a leaking roof, mowing the lawn or painting dirty walls" give the material a virility suitable for its context.

A SHORT DEVOTIONAL

He was a very ordinary-looking man walking along the sidewalk. It was at the close of day but darkness had not yet begun to spread its mantle everywhere. About three feet from the curbstone, a group of birds was pecking away at a small opening in the side of a pink paper bag. They were quarreling as they pecked because there must have been many suggestions being offered as to the best way to get to the crumbs that were hidden there. The man walked over to the spot; the birds took rapid flight, settling at a respectful distance in the grass, watching. With his foot he turned the bag over, examined it with some care, then reached down and emptied the bag and its contents of bread crumbs. When he had done this, he resumed his walk. As soon as he disappeared, the birds returned to find that a miracle had taken place. Instead of a bag full of hidden crumbs, only a glimpse of which they had seen, there was before them now a full abundance for satisfying their need. The man had gone on his way without even a backward glance. Of course he could have walked away casting his glances back to feast his eyes on the results of his efforts. Or he could have withdrawn far enough so as not to disturb the birds, and watched them eat while he congratulated himself because he was kind to birds and extremely sensitive to their needs. But he did none of these things. He went on his way without even a backward glance. Any careful scrutiny of one's own life will reveal the fact that we have been in the predicament of the birds again and again. The thing one needed was somewhat in evidence but out of reach. With all of one's resources, one worked away at the opening, trying first one attack and then another; then some stranger, some unknown writer, some passing comment from another, did the needful thing. We are all of us indebted to a vast host of anonymous persons without whom some necessity would not have been available, some good which came to us, we would have missed. It is not too far-fetched to say that living is itself an act of interdependence. However strong we may be or think we are, we are constantly leaning on others. However self-sufficient we are, our strength is always being supplied by others unknown to us whose paths led them down our street or by our house at the moment that we needed the light they could give. We are all of us the birds and we are all of us the man. It is the way of life; it is one of the means by which God activates Himself in the texture of human life and human experience.[5]

Note:

• The first sentence plunges us into a narrative. We are intrigued and read on.
• Use of descriptive phrases: "spread its mantle," "pecking away," "quarreling as they pecked," "took rapid flight, settling at a respectful distance," "casting his glances back," "worked away at the opening," "leaning on others."
• The whole has a simplicity befitting a meditation: the act around which it is built is simple, the sentences are simple, the point is simple.
• In the short space given, the author presses toward only one goal or thought, the truth expressed in the last sentence.
• The account contains subtle humor, subtle psychological insight, subtle theology. It means more than it says and thus furnishes genuine grist for meditation.

● Only one "this" occurs in the whole account.

SUMMARY

No, not all of the passages you read were written by professional writers. Most of them were done by amateurs who were so caught up in their message that they set themselves to tell it well. They held the driving thought in check long enough to put it down in an orderly, clear, restrained but powerful fashion. They gave their works economy, energy, and subtlety!

Checklist

Here are two checklists: One you may use before you begin to compose your message; the other you may use after you have written it.

BEFORE

1. Is your goal clear and specific?
2. Have you fixed your audience or readers in mind?
3. Are you coming to them as a know-it-all or as a fellow human?
4. Have you gleaned enough material so that you can incarnate your message, telling it in terms of people (if possible)?
5. Are you setting aside adequate time to organize your ideas and to find just the right words to express them? Especially enough time if your assignment is brief?

AFTER

1. As your eye falls over the page, do any colorful words or names of people and places stand out?
2. Is your first sentence short?
3. Is the first sentence interesting?

4. Does it begin with "There is" or "There was" or "It is" or "It was"? If so, change it.
5. Is the first paragraph interesting?
6. Have you used strong, descriptive verbs? Do "is" and "was" appear time and again?
7. How many "have's" and "has's" choke the pages?
8. Have you overworked "this," "that," "these," and "those"? Especially "this"?
9. Is there an obvious antecedent for every pronoun?
10. Are your clauses parallel?
11. Have you used present tense wherever possible?
12. Have you served as eyes, ears, and nose for your reader, telling him what happened in concrete (raw) terms?
13. How many words can you eliminate from the account without destroying its thought or power?
14. Will the finished message fit well in its context?
15. Would you yourself like to read or hear it?

Notes

Introduction

1. "Jack Paar: A New Approach," *Look,* Vol. 26, No. 21 (October 9, 1962), p. 93.
2. *The Interpreter's Bible,* Vol. VII, edited by George Buttrick (New York and Nashville: Abingdon-Cokesbury Press, 1951), p. 408.
3. Magazine Section, *New York Times* (January 24, 1960), p. 43.
4. Paul Scherer, *For We Have This Treasure: The Yale Lectures on Preaching, 1943* (New York: Harper & Brothers, Publishers, 1944), pp. 144-145. Italics mine.
5. J. B. Phillips, *Making Men Whole* (New York: The Macmillan Company, 1955), p. 44.

Chapter One

1. Colossians 4:6.
2. Joyce Cary, *Except the Lord* (New York: Harper & Brothers, 1953), p. 88.
3. Oliver Goldsmith, *The Vicar of Wakefield* (New York: Cassell, Peter, Galpin and Co., 1885), p. 83.
4. J. Donald Adams, *The Shape of Books to Come* (New York: The Viking Press, 1944), p. 55.
5. *The Interpreter's Bible, op. cit.,* p. 408.
6. Matthew 23:27, King James Version.
7. Han Suyin, "Shanghai," *Holiday,* Vol. 30, No. 2 (August 1961), pp. 61, 80.

Chapter Two

1. Thomas Godfrey, "The Prince of Parthia," *Representative American Plays from 1787 to the Present,* edited by Arthur Hobson Quinn (New York: D. Appleton-Century Company, 1938), p. 37.

2. Norman G. Shidle, *Clear Writing for Easy Reading* (New York: McGraw-Hill Book Company, Inc., 1951), p. 85.

3. Thomas Hardy, *Far From the Madding Crowd* (New York: Harper and Brothers, 1901), p. 254.

4. Baxter Hathaway, *Writing Mature Prose* (New York: The Ronald Press Co., 1951), p. 11.

5. Charles Horton Cooley, *Life and the Student* (New York: Alfred A. Knopf, 1927), p. 81. Italics mine.

6. *Reader's Digest* (September 1961), pp. 111-112.

7. George Rice Hovey, *Christian Ethics for Daily Life* (New York: Association Press, 1932), p. 54.

8. *Pittsburgh Sun-Telegraph* (April 30, 1957), p. 21.

9. Quoted in the *New York Times* (January 2, 1960), p. 22.

10. Sara Henderson Hay, *The Stone and the Shell* (Pittsburgh: The University of Pittsburgh Press, 1959), jacket cover.

11. Anne Morrow Lindbergh, *Gift from the Sea* (New York: Pantheon Books, Inc., 1955), jacket cover.

12. "Summer and Winter," *Poems with Power to Strengthen the Soul* compiled and edited by James Mudge (New York and Nashville: Abingdon Press, 1907), p. 54.

Chapter Three

1. Catherine Marshall, "My Life Since *A Man Called Peter*," *McCall's*, Vol. LXXX, No. 11 (August 1953), p. 108.

2. *Pittsburgh Sun-Telegraph* (April 30, 1957), p. 21.

3. Paul Scherer, *For We Have This Treasure*, p. 188.

4. James E. Sellers, *The Outsider and the Word of God:* A study in Christian communication (New York and Nashville: Abingdon Press, 1961), p. 227.

5. George Arthur Buttrick, *Sermons Preached in a University Church* (New York and Nashville: Abingdon Press, 1959), p. 124.

6. Lucille Ball, as told to Leonard Slater, "The Way It Happened," *McCall's,* Vol. LXXXVII, No. 12 (September 1960), p. 215.

7. Mildred E. Whitcomb, "My Journey Through Doubt," *These Found the Way,* edited by David Wesley Soper (Philadelphia: The Westminster Press, 1951), p. 29.

8. Webb B. Garrison, *Why You Say It* (New York and Nashville: Abingdon Press, 1955), pp. 202, 203.

9. Edith Ogutsch, quoted in "Toward More Picturesque Speech," *Reader's Digest,* Vol. 79, No. 475 (November 1961), p. 193.

10. Cf. "The Mammoth Mirror," *Time,* Vol. LXXX, No. 15 (October 12, 1962), p. 85.

Chapter Four

1. Freeman Wills Crofts, *The Four Gospels in One Story* (New York: Longmans, Green and Co, 1949), p. 158.
2. St. Francis, "The Canticle of the Creatures," *A Diary of Readings,* edited by John Baillie (New York: Charles Scribner's Sons, 1955), Day 27.
3. J. B. Phillips, *Your God Is Too Small* (New York: The Macmillan Company, 1962), p. 20.
4. Quoted in Howard Tillman Kuist, *These Words Upon Thy Heart* (Richmond, Va.: John Knox Press, 1947), p. 68.
5. Luke 6:38.
6. J. B. Phillips, *Appointment with God* (New York: The Macmillan Company, 1957), p. 20.
7. Proverbs 26:11.
8. Lewis Joseph Sherrill, *Guilt and Redemption* (Richmond, Va.: John Knox Press, 1945), p. 173.

Chapter Five

1. Hazen G. Werner, *Christian Family Living* (New York and Nashville: Abingdon Press, 1958), p. 120.
2. A. W. Beaven, *The Fine Art of Living Together* (New York: Harper & Brothers, 1927), p. 144.
3. Helmut Thielicke, *The Waiting Father,* translated by John W. Doberstein (New York: Harper & Row, Publishers, 1959), pp. 65, 144, 55, 141, 57, 76.
4. Matthew 5:39.
5. Paul Scherer, *Event in Eternity* (New York: Harper & Brothers Publishers, 1945), p. 224.
6. George Arthur Buttrick, *Prayer* (New York and Nashville: Abingdon Press, 1942), p. 149.
7. George S. Stewart, *The Lower Levels of Prayer* (New York and Nashville: Abingdon Press, 1940), p. 17.
8. Donald Hankey, "From the Trenches," *A Diary of Readings,* op. cit., Day 34.
9. Emil Brunner, *Our Faith* (New York: Charles Scribner's Sons, 1954), p. 88.
10. C. S. Lewis, *George Macdonald: An Anthology* (New York: The Macmillan Company, 1948), p. 70.
11. Scherer, *For We Have This Treasure,* p. 71.
12. Buttrick, *Prayer,* p. 210.
13. Scherer, *Event in Eternity,* p. 67.
14. Psalm 23:1.

15. John 11:25.

16. Psalm 46:5.

17. John 3:16. Italics mine.

18. Romans 6:8. Italics mine.

19. John 4:13, 14. Italics mine.

20. Esther 4:14. Italics mine.

21. Luke 20:25.

22. Book-of-the-Month Club advertisement.

23. Shidle, *Clear Writing for Easy Reading*, p. 58.

24. J. B. Phillips, *Plain Christianity and Other Broadcast Talks* (New York: The Macmillan Company, 1954), p. 75.

25. "Stirring Salute to Valor," *Life*, Vol. 52 (January 12, 1962), p. 55. Italics mine.

Chapter Six

1. Quoted in Lawrence Langer, "Mean More Than You Say," *Theatre Arts*, Vol. XXXVII, No. 7 (July 1953), p. 29.

2. Luke 14:11.

3. Keith G. Huntress, Albert L. Walker, Robert B. Orlovich, Barriss Mills, *Minimum Essentials for Good Writing* (Boston: D. C. Heath & Co., 1962), p. 42.

4. *The Journal of Gamaliel Bradford*, edited by Van Wyck Brooks (New York: Houghton Mifflin Co., 1933), p. 274.

5. Quoted in Wilbur M. Smith, *Therefore, Stand* (Boston: W. A. Wilde Co., 1945), p. 476.

6. Luke 10:29-30, 33-34, 36.

7. Luke 15:8-10.

8. Antoine de Saint Exupéry, *Wind, Sand and Stars* (New York: Bantam Books, 1945), p. 236.

Chapter Seven

1. Reprinted from *David the King* by Gladys Schmitt. Copyright 1946 by Gladys Schmitt and used with the permission of the publishers, The Dial Press.

2. *College Themes*, Department of English, University of Pittsburgh (Pittsburgh: University of Pittsburgh Press, 1943), p. 63.

3. From the Pennies, Kampala, Uganda (February 1, 1961).

4. A. S. Tippit, "Weekly Sermonette," *Richmond News Leader* (April 21, 1962).

5. Howard Thurman, *Meditations of the Heart* (New York: Harper & Brothers, Publishers, 1953), pp. 130-132.

40377   808.06
                                              N51

Date Due

**NYACK MISSIONARY COLLEGE
NYACK, NEW YORK**

PRINTED IN U.S.A.